Collecting
TOY SOLDIERS

Collecting
TOY SOLDIERS

JAMES OPIE

New Cavendish Books
London

Pincushion Press
Tampa

DEDICATION

For all my collecting friends, especially Jeremy de Souza with whom I war-gamed as a boy; also Ed Ruby, Scott Morlan, Jim Poulton, David Bracey, Edmund Roche-Kelly, Len Richards, Richard Lane, Barrie Blood, Norman Joplin, Shamus Wade, Ged Haley, John Garratt, Jan and Frank Scroby, John Tunstill, Peter Cowan, Roland Bamford, John Ruddle, Peter Johnson, Cyril Couts, Giles Brown, Donald Pudney, Arnold Rolac, Freddie Green, Roy Dilley, George Palmer, Bill Pierce, James Luck, Frank Perry, John Teychener, Colin Barber, Neil Crowley, Kemble Widmer, Steve Balchin, Pierce Carlson, Gus Hanson, Burtt Ehrlich, Joe Wallis Jo and Steve Sommers , Jack Jenkinson, John Norris Wood, Brian Harrison, Peter Flateau, Andrew Rose, David Pierce, Ernie Marshall, Alex Riches, John Franklin, Jenney Burley, Roy Selwyn-Smith, Charles Biggs, Paul Collet, Ken Pizey and many more who make the hobby fun to live with, as well as finally my wife Mary, who collected me.

Text © James Opie 1987
Collective work
© New Cavendish Books 1992

First published in hardback 1987
by William Collins
Paperback edition first published
in 1992 by New Cavendish Books

Printed and bound in China
Produced by Mandarin Offset

New Cavendish Books Ltd.
3 Denbigh Road
London W11 2SJ

ISBN 1 872727 76 X

Published in the USA by
Pincushion Press
5245 Baywater Drive
Tampa, FL 33615

FORNTISPIECE

In 1936 Britains and the British Model Soldier Society started a joint project to produce the British infantry and Highlander troops at Waterloo to put opposite the many toys produced on the continent of First Empire French and the other nations. These sets were released by Britains in its regular range in 1937 and stayed in the catalogue until 1959. The infantry usually had grey trousers, although sometimes they were issued in blue. To the right of the group are shown unpainted castings as they were supplied to members of the Society to paint up for the project. Later in the 1950s, the figures were redesigned with a single movable arm (rather than two) and an artillery set was added. Enterprising collectors would convert other Britains troops to Waterloo period, as with the marching infantry and Scots Greys at the back (**g**). Author's collection

RIGHT

Britains set 2, the Royal Horse Guards second version, in which the soldiers have tin swords, in its original early box (l,i). There is a casting fault in the plume of the second figure from the right, but most collectors would not consider this a defect. Phillips

CONTENTS

FOREWORD

The Collectors' Centre at Phillips has built its reputation upon making available to buyers and sellers alike the very best service and expertise in specialist collectables of a relatively modest value. Phillips are unquestionably the largest auctioneers of toy soldiers in the world, starting their specialized sales as early as 1970. Since then an unbroken series of sales devoted to toy soldiers has enjoyed massive support and proved that collectors worldwide are passionately inspired to improve their displays. Toy soldiers continue to be the largest individual subject area within the toy collecting province.

Over the past seven years we have been fortunate to enjoy the services and general advice and guidance of James Opie as consultant valuer on toy soldiers. He has been a prominent collector and researcher of toy soldiers for very many years, and we believe that his knowledge of his subject is unrivalled in his chosen field. The toy soldier is now ranked alongside the military miniature as an object for collecting and leisure interest, and that it is so is in no small part due to his efforts.

ANDREW HILTON
Director, Collectors' Centre,
Phillips Auctioneers

INTRODUCTION

This book has been a joy to write, as it has given me an opportunity to demonstrate all the pleasure that I have derived from collecting toy soldiers. I make no apology for including a certain amount of auto-biography, for I have dabbled happily in various aspects of the hobby. My purpose is that, in reading of my experiences, others may be encouraged to try this fascinating hobby for themselves and enjoy similar rewards. By far the greater number of the examples discussed and illustrated are of British hollow-cast toys, since they are what I have concentrated on collecting, but collectors who prefer other types will find it easy to translate the principles suggested into their own terms, and for the beginner I have included in Chapter 2 a brief summary of the various options open to collectors.

I was given my first toy soldiers when I was four years old. My grandmother's carpenter kindly cast a dozen cavalry in peak caps from a home casting mould: they were semi-flat, solid lead and extremely heavy, about 2½in (64mm) tall. My grandmother painted the horses brown and the men red from two tins of enamel from the ironmongers. I was hooked.

Later my aunt gave me a box of Britains' second-grade hussars and infantry on guard, bought at Barkers of Kensington. My other grand-mother took me to the local toyshop and asked me to choose. The choice narrowed down to a large mixed set of Crescent soldiers and an EverReady toy underground train set. In a momentous decision, the toy soldiers won (although I have had nostalgic moments of regret for the train), and a cardboard fort was added to the booty to make the value up to a suitable present. The next sally was to Harrods, where my grandmother purchased for me my first set of Britains' best quality toy soldiers. I thought at the time they were Foot Guards, but in reality they were Royal Welch Fusiliers. My first cavalry box was the Royal Scots Greys, with headgear that looked like the Fusiliers', and these two regiments remain my favourites.

From the start, my toy soldiers played war-games, usually the "goodies" versus the "baddies". The baddies would invade the goodies and kill them off until the best goodie troops arrived in the nick of time and defeated them. I already had a good idea of how wars of aggression were played out in real life. Later, all my troops defended the bedroom of my grandmother's flat against an invasion by a friend down the road. This developed into a series of contests between our imaginary countries, Magmania and Superland. So that we could build up distinguishable armies, we agreed that the regiments of toy soldiers used in one army would not be purchased by the other, and we were soon scouring the toyshops for figures that were not yet reserved for the other side.

As I grew up, so my interest in the variety of toy soldiers grew and blossomed, receiving an especial boost when I joined the British Model Soldier Society (B.M.S.S.) at the then minimum age of 18. Although I was already buying any soldiers that were attractive and within my means, I found that most collectors already possessed good collections of metal figures, particularly those by Britains, so I concentrated on what was little collected at that time – contemporary plastic toy figures. In this I was greatly encouraged by Len Richards, who inspired me to collect more systematically.

With some diversion into 1/1200 scale ship models and 1/72 scale war-gaming, I concentrated on collecting plastic figures until I moved back to London in 1970 and started to build up the hollow-cast side of my collection, mainly through the auctions at Phillips. In 10 years, I acquired what I felt was a satisfactory representation of all British-made toy soldiers manufactured between 1893 and 1973.

Having achieved this, I was able to take a rather more relaxed view of collecting. I became consultant cataloguer at Phillips and wrote the catalogues for the sale of the Richards and Hanington collections. More recently, I have been trying to pass on my enjoyment to others in the form of books, of which this is the fourth.

My collection has declined somewhat in numbers since 1980, and I have concentrated on the more unusual items rather than trying to possess examples of everything. I have had more time to appreciate the display and converting sides of the hobby, and this culminated in my exhibition at the London Toy and Model Museum, where for the whole of 1985 I was given the opportunity of showing my collecting philosophy to visitors.

This book is an attempt to share the knowledge about how to collect that I have acquired during the past 40 years. I hope that anyone with a problem will find an answer in this text. I hope too, that newcomers to the hobby will find it useful to follow the three principles upon which I now collect: first, that the collection should satisfy a sense of intellectual curiosity; second, that it should recall as many pleasant collecting memories as possible; and third, that my collection should be aesthetically pleasing to me (although my taste is not everyone's, and I find myself being increasingly influenced by my wife, Mary, with undoubtedly beneficial effect). My object is to enjoy shaping a unique collection.

1
WHAT IS A TOY SOLDIER?

A toy soldier is a military model that is used as a plaything by children. Commercial toy soldiers are manufactured *en masse* and distributed through the toy trade. Mass-produced toys of all sorts were one of the benefits of the industrial revolution, and toy soldiers were among the earliest toys to be made and were widely distributed from the early 19th century.

Collectors of these toys distinguish their hobby from that of the military modeller, who collects miniatures, as lifelike as possible, that depict warlike subjects. The distinction between a toy soldier and a model soldier is not easy to maintain clearly, since all the toys are models of soldiers, and even the most intricate model can be used as a plaything. Many toy soldiers are actually quite good models, and many models are distributed through the commercial toy market. Models can be quite sturdy; toys can be fragile. Intricacy of detail or accuracy can be associated with toys as much as with models. Perhaps it is up to collectors to decide by consensus which figures fall into which category, although the manufacturer's intention to supply children or adults is a major consideration.

The main characteristics of toy soldiers are that the degree of accuracy varies from manufacturer to manufacturer; they tend to be simple in decoration; they are mass produced and distributed through toyshops; and they are traditionally available ready painted.

Model soldiers, on the other hand, are extremely accurately made or the manufacturer has made an attempt to achieve a high degree of accuracy; they are intricately moulded; they are either unique models or made in short production runs; they are distributed via mail order or through model shops; and they are usually sold unpainted.

Children use toy soldiers in their play worlds over which they have complete control. Toy soldiers can be lined up for shooting games, opposed to each other for war-games or used for endless opposition to heroes operating invincibly against impossible odds and so on. But in spite of the emphasis on actively playing with their toys, many children nevertheless value their appearance and treasure them faithfully throughout their use. The more magnificent the toys were when new, the more they are likely to have survived, possibly because their impressive appearance instilled a certain degree of awe. This explains why so many of the shoddier, second-grade and plastic figures have failed to survive,

This Ping model is of a French knight shot by an arrow at the battle of Poitiers. Courtenay knights are even more sought after by toy soldiers collectors and are among the few highly detailed models that are valued in this way. The knight illustrated here is worth about £50 (j), while Courtenays fetch between £100 and £500. *Phillips*

and these are now curiosities to the collector who researches everything produced, although they are as unappealing as ever to the collector who prefers more artistic items.

The adult collector may never have stopped collecting from his youth, but it is more usual for a period of adolescent interest in other things to have interrupted the hobby before an adult tries to recapture the youthful pleasure of playing with soldiers. Nostalgia for childhood is one of the strongest reasons for collecting. Another is an admiration for toy soldiers as miniature works of art. As with most art, some examples are better than others, but with toys, as opposed to models, the basic simplicity is always there. Military miniatures often attempt too much realism and overwhelm the aesthetic effect.

Maybe the toy soldier collector is a potential dictator, shut away in a cellar with thousands of warlike toys – as H. G. Wells would have dealt with all such people. Certainly, there is a sort of power to be experienced

This Military Band of the Seaforth Highlanders was from the Hanington collection. These are, technically, model soldiers, since they are Rose castings with "Eyes Right" instruments, and the whole band has been painted with matt paints in an attempt to give greater realism. However, the simple design of the figures gives an effect similar to the best toy soldiers and demonstrates the blurred distinction between the two hobbies. This very attractive model, which fetched £340 in 1984, is now in the Forbes collection (J).
Phillips

A proper toy knight, probably by Heyde, in a large 65mm scale, this figure is worth about £50 (j). Solid cast, it was made in Germany about 1900. *Phillips*

Britains souvenirs of the coronation of King George VI – *item 1473*, King George VI in coronation robe (**h**), *item 1474*, the coronation chair (**f**) and *item 1506*, Queen Elizabeth (**h**) – are on a rather larger scale than Britains normal 54mm. *Phillips*

in reviewing endless ranks of soldiers. But there is a great deal more comfort to be gained in thinking that none of these toys will ever be sent on a warlike mission. The purpose of collecting is more to assemble decorative tableaux depicting events and parades, to record the astonishing diversity of such toys in the past, to complete a particular plan of acquisition, or simply to own a satisfying quantity of charming and evocative toy figures.

There are additional ways of taking the hobby further: some collectors research the uniforms and history of the soldiers represented, others prefer to learn of the enterprises that brought all these models to the market place, and a great deal of scholarly research into the manufacturers of unattributed figures has yet to be done. I try to attach a story to each group of figures in my collection, using it to illustrate part of the history of toy soldier manufacturing or the contemporary wars and their effect on the toy makers.

Toy soldiers are (in 1987) in plentiful supply to be collected. They are valuable enough to make them worth selling by people who do not collect, but not so valuable that only the wealthy can afford them. Storing away a collection of toy soldiers satisfies any squirrel instinct, and, in terms of value, has proved at least as good a hedge against inflation as most other possessions.

The best part of collecting toy soldiers, however, is that they can be brought out and actively enjoyed. Artistic impulses can be satisfied by the moulding, converting and painting of new models, or by the repair and restoration of old ones. Meeting fellow collectors is a means of making many friends and provides an endless source of conversation among congenial company. Whatever stage your collection reaches, it will be an extension of your personality, and from it you can show, as an art form, any favourite exhibit, to share with friends and neighbours worldwide.

2
A SHORT HISTORY OF TOY SOLDIERS

Mankind has always had the urge to reproduce his environment. From the earliest times, attempts to understand the world have included the creation of models, closely followed by the provision of toys for growing children.

TOY SOLDIERS IN ANTIQUITY

The earliest surviving "toy armies" are those that were entombed with rulers on the religious understanding that in the afterlife they would be symbolic of the status of the person with whom they were buried. Notable examples of this are the tombs of the Pharoahs of Egypt, soldiers from which are to be found in the British Museum, and the life-size figures found in recent excavations in China.

In the tombs of children and in archaeological sites all over the ancient world terracotta or lead figures have been found, the metal ones being moulded in a very similar fashion to the semi-flat models made in Germany thousands of years later. The late John G. Garratt, in his book *Model Soldiers: A Collector's Guide*, put together a comprehensively sourced article on these early figures, which has not been bettered in any subsequent publication. This evidence of a universal interest in military models and toys is significant because it shows that such items are a deeply rooted symptom of human civilization, rather than merely a newly discovered expression of our modern age. Most modern collectors, however, although interested in such antiquities, do not regard them as collectable objects, limiting themselves instead to the commercially made toys produced after the industrial revolution of the 19th century.

During the Middle Ages, models were used for more practical purposes than in earlier times. Complete suits of miniature armour and jousting toys have survived, and these obviously had a practical purpose beyond that of being children's playthings. The education of soldiers was furthered by the use of instructional models, often made out of precious metals, showing all aspects of warfare. The tradition of making the humbler lead or pottery figures also continued, right up until the manufacturers of such figures first attempted mass production.

FLATS

Although man's basic urge to produce miniature soldier figures is well attested by the discovery of artefacts dating from all periods, commer-

These flat figures of knights in armour were made by Besold of Nuremberg, possibly as early as 1830. Unusual features of these fine 65mm flats are the movable arms and visors. These two were sold for £140 at Phillips in 1987 (**k**). *Phillips*

RIGHT
Examples of the normal modern size of flat figures, 28mm scale, the most popular scale for flats since 1880 (**a**). Top row: the British staff officer at Waterloo on the left is painted in matt colour, as modern collectors of flats usually prefer – the rest are in the manufacturers' original glossy toy finish, which often lets the bare metal shine through the paint to give a metallic effect.

The other two rows seen here show an assortment of the Authenticast and Swedish African Engineers figures designed by Holger Eriksson (**c**). Some I enjoy more than others, but, with few exceptions, the standard of modelling is high and, at the time they were produced (from 1946 onwards), they were forerunners of the military miniature rather than in the tradition of the toy soldier. My favourites are the Cameron

cially produced toy soldiers were first distributed during the 18th century. These were flat, tin figures, originating in Germany. After they had been produced for a hundred years, the firm of Ernst Heinrichsen of Nuremberg became pre-eminent and established a standard scale of about 30mm* tall for infantrymen, although many pieces are somewhat shorter than this.

Flat figures are so called because of their two-dimensional nature. Usually less than 1mm thick, they are cast in slate moulds and look like little metal cut-outs. They are often beautifully engraved on each side, showing a front and back view of the soldier. At first they were sold, unpainted, by weight – an ounce box of figures would contain as many soldiers as could be made out of an ounce of tin. German manufacturers have always been the source of most flat figures, and after two and a half centuries in production, they are still made in that country in great variety.

During the latter half of the 19th century, many sets of flats in small wooden or cardboard boxes were exported from Germany to Britain, where there was at that time no indigenous manufacturing. In France, however, where some flats and other types were being made, the Germans did not achieve the same success. In Britain, therefore, flats dating back to 1850 or earlier are often to be found, some in the

*The scales used by manufacturers are discussed on pages 80–1.

manufacturer's original paint and boxes. During the period 1900–60 in English-speaking countries the popularity of flat soldiers was eclipsed by that of other types of toy soldier, and so items painted by the manufacturer are not common. However, because few collectors are interested in them, those that become available are not expensive.

Since 1960, a growing number of enthusiasts have found the collecting, casting and re-casting of flats a fascinating hobby, the main attraction residing in the incredible detail of the cast features. Most collectors buy unpainted castings or cast their own, and lavish their skills on the most intricate paintwork. The activity is more akin to model soldiering, and the modern, expertly painted flats are a world apart from the 19th-century toys. Toy makers used gloss paint rather than the matt finish preferred by most modern artists, and often the paint appears translucent as the metal shines through the thin, oil-based enamels that were used.

The paintwork of some manufacturers even then showed first-class detail, and the qualities of the paint give the figures a look almost as if they were cut out of a stained-glass window, an appearance that, even though it is different from that of any other type of toy soldier, is just as aesthetically pleasing. As an art form, the toy soldier could have been said to have attained its apogee at the first attempt.

Collecting these old flat toy soldiers is extremely difficult, since the makers' marks are scarce, catalogues are confusing or non-existent, and the main works of reference are in German. Certain very well known sets,

Highlanders from World War I at the left of the centre row and the pikeman at the other end of the same row. The fifth figure from the right in the centre row is a recently produced volunteer corps officer made in Australia, and the fourth figure from the right in that row is a Prussian infantryman of the Franco-Prussian War by Quality Model Toys. These figures show how the influence of Eriksson's style of rugged sculptured modelling has continued to be felt. The mounted figure on the right of the bottom row is plastic, one of the figures produced by Malleable Mouldings in 1947, also to Eriksson's designs. *Author's collection*

however, are highly valued and greatly sought after. For example, Heinrichsen's set, Alexander the Great and the Persians, which contains 360 figures, is worth about £2,000.

SOLIDS

Solid toy soldiers – solids – are simply fully round models, cast in solid metal. The French were the pioneers of this sort of toy soldier, although metal workers and jewellers in most countries often made miniature figures from precious materials. About the time of the French Revolution and Napoleon I, the regular manufacture of toy soldiers began in Paris,

and the scale used was similar to the scale that has since proved most popular – i.e., 54mm scale.

Although very few toys still exist from this early period, several manufacturers traced their origins back to this time. The only major company to survive today is Mignot, which gradually swallowed up all the others by a succession of mergers, including, most notably, that with Lucotte. French manufacturers have always tended to concentrate primarily on the First Empire period and then on French historical types, with patriotism and a desire to satisfy the home market the prime considerations. Mignot figures are widely collected today, although they

These finely detailed, solid-cast Lucottes from the Hanington collection were made in France, and they depict French soldiers of the First Empire period. They are highly sought after and cost about £50 per figure (**k**). The mounted figures would be two or three times more costly (**m**). *Phillips*

The poses of these solid-cast Heyde nurses and wounded soldiers (**h**) from the field hospital set (illustrated opposite) are typically elaborate for toys, compared with the rather more inactive Britains medical figures. The four horse-drawn vehicles, tent, trees and so forth of the field hospital set are in 50mm scale, which is slightly smaller than the scale commonly used by Britains. The variety of action poses is considerable, and the hospital tents, beds and bedding can be carried on the vehicles. John Hanington, from whose collection this fine set came, made a speciality of medical subjects within his otherwise wide-ranging collection. This set, now in the Forbes collection, was purchased for £2,800 in 1984 (**M**). *Phillips*

are expensive to buy, and the somewhat superior figures by Lucotte are rare and costly.

In Germany, a number of firms started to make solid figures around the middle of the 19th century, and, as with other German toys, a strong export trade was quickly established. Among the many manufacturers, Heyde of Dresden was foremost, with Haffner and Heinrich also prominent. Because their style is so distinctive, a collection of German-made solids is both interesting and coherent.

Characteristically, German solids were made of soft lead, and they were basic figures that could be dressed in the uniform of any of the world's armies. Equipment and heads were cast separately and added as appropriate. They were made in any size from 20mm scale to 120mm scale, and, although the most common size was 45mm scale, no one size was so dominant that it could be regarded as the norm. The soft lead could be twisted into a wide variety of animated postures, and often little scenes were set up with two or three figures on a tinplate base. Tinplate was used also for vehicles, guns and scenery.

In the larger sizes, the metal used tended to be harder, and the greater thickness gave the figures more strength. As a rule, the larger the figure, the more detailed was the painting and moulding, and details even included such features as moustaches, the painting often rivalling that on the dolls made by the same toy industry.

As with German flats, the variety was enormous. Heyde in particular was willing to produce almost any figure to order in any of five different scales and many sizes of box. The company's catalogue offers all possible combinations rather than a list of standard sets, which makes collecting by catalogue number extremely difficult.

These 48mm German troops by Heyde depict the times of Frederick the Great, and German manufacturers particularly enjoyed making toy soldiers from this formative time in German history. These examples from the Hanington collection have considerable charm (**h**). *Phillips*

In Britain and the United States, German solid figures enjoyed their greatest popularity from 1880 to 1914, and Heyde and Heinrich had the best agents and the widest distribution. From 1897 in Britain, however, the distribution of these toys decreased as the popularity of Britains' hollow-cast figures increased. Britains was able to undercut German prices by as much as 50 per cent.

At their best German solid figures are highly individual and artistic. They are fluidly posed and meticulously painted, and although the high lead content in the figures makes them especially prone to oxydization, many collectors find that they cannot resist owning some of the more interesting pieces.

SEMI-FLATS

Compared with flats, solid figures are difficult to mould, so a hybrid style of toy soldier quickly evolved. Known as semi-flats, or sometimes semi-solids, they are a cross between the two: figures in bas-relief, up to 10 times the thickness of the true flat, yet no more than half-way towards an all-round representation. The deeper relief allowed a reasonable impression of a soldier to be achieved with less painstaking engraving and painting than was necessary with a true flat, but the figures were still a great deal easier to cast than the solids.

These advantages lent themselves to the manufacture of inferior products cast out of the cheapest metal, and these are what are usually to be found. So easy is the casting of these figures, that firms set themselves up to distribute moulds for home casting, and many of the resulting soldiers may be found in attics. They are sometimes brought to auction houses for valuation, but they are worthless; even the moulds themselves have hardly any value. Lately, Prinz August, a Swedish firm, has been issuing semi-flat home casting models, but more recently it has embarked on fully round and war-game moulds.

MODERN SOLIDS

Since the demise of Britains' hollow-cast toy soldiers in 1966, the solid-cast toy soldier has seen something of a revival. Centrifugal moulding with inexpensive, vulcanized rubber moulds has enabled manufacturers to produce short runs economically, and many small firms have started up in both Britain and the United States to cater for the modern collector of toy soldiers. The prevailing trend has been to extend the number of collectables by reproducing the style of the old "true" toy soldier while in general not attempting to make an exact replica. Some companies have been more successful than others, either in striking out with a distinctive style or collecting theme of their own, or in adding figures compatible with Britains in poses not produced by the original manufacturer. Some of the products of these new toy soldier manufacturers are already out of production and sought after by collectors just as avidly as older toy models.

OVERLEAF
This beautiful two-tier box containing British Army staff and officers was made by Heyde about 1910, and it was once the property of Prince John, son of George V. These German toy soldiers are solid cast in 52mm scale, and the painting shows great attention to detail (**L, j**). *Phillips*

Assorted figures designed by Holger Eriksson for Authenticast; these were solid cast and made in Eire (**c**). *Phillips*

OPPOSITE ABOVE
All the figures in this illustration – with one exception – are by unknown manufacturers. The exception is the cowboy in the centre, which is an unusual fixed-arm, best quality figure by Britains (**i**). All the figures are hollow-cast and are likely to have been made in Britain. Note the two Guards (second and third from left, top row) in greatcoats, one of which has been mistakenly painted in red (**c**). *Author's collection*

OPPOSITE BELOW
On the left is a French-made band of hollow-cast figures (**C**), this method of manufacture having seemingly taken root in France during the existence of Britains Paris Office and factory. Notice that the puttees of the horn player are a different colour from those of the rest of the band, which might lead one to suspect that it did not originally belong to this set. On the right is a drum and bugle band of the French Parachutists, with officers, rank and file (**C, e**). These are typical of the aluminium figures produced by Quiralu. When plastic soldiers were introduced by others in competition, Quiralu produced this set, among others, in plastic as well. *Author's collection*

As with toy producing firms in former years, new toy soldier manufacturers have tended to be small and transient. Some notable examples are: Blenheim, William Hocker, Ducal, Steadfast, All the Queen's Men, Bastion, Mark Time, Bulldog, Imperial Productions, Trophy and Dorset.

HOLLOW-CAST

Hollow-cast toy soldiers were invented by the Britain family and first went into production in 1893 in London, England. The process involves pouring an antimony-rich alloy rapidly into and out of a mould so that a hollow figure is formed when the still-hot metal is poured out of the centre of the mould, while the cooler metal that has set round the edges is left.

The method was commercially successful because less metal was needed than to make a fully rounded figure and so the raw material costs were much lower. Britains toy soldiers swept the market in Britain over a period of five years, but then had to compete with a multitude of home-bred competitors using the same process. None came close to equalling the quality, consistency of product or output of Britains, which continually improved the figures it produced and maintained its lead. German firms also attempted to use the hollow-cast method, with mixed results, and from about 1920 onwards, hollow-casts were produced in France and America (*see also* dime-store figures, page 32). Later the process was used throughout the world. Because of the widespread success of Britains in the export market and the consistent numbering system of its catalogue, the output of this firm is by far the most widely collected, although the number of collectors is not great in continental Europe, where people tend to prefer their indigenous product.

Britains produced hollow-cast figures between 1893 and 1966, and this production was punctuated by the two world wars, during both of which the company turned to munitions production. It is thus convenient to consider the production of Britains' toys in three major periods: before World War I, between the wars and after World War II.

Before World War I the main rivals to Britains in hollow-cast manufacture were: Reka (C. W. Baker), Abel and Renvoize; between the world wars they were: B.M.C. (Britannia Model Company), Crescent, John Hill & Co. and Taylor & Barratt; and after World War II they were: Timpo, John Hill & Co., Crescent, Charbens and Cherilea. Of these companies, only Timpo and Hill made serious efforts to export, mostly to the United States.

COMPOSITION TOY SOLDIERS

Composition is a mixture of sawdust and various gluey substances, such as casein, kneaded into a sort of dough, which is squeezed around a wire skeleton into a mould and baked to make it hard before painting. The result is a light, tough toy, which tends to chip like plaster if roughly handled. The process was first used around the start of the 20th century as an extension of doll manufacturing.

The most famous and widely distributed composition manufactured toys were by Hausser, with its trademark Elastolin (the company's name

These French infantry of the line figures are 100mm scale, and they were made by the French toy manufacturer S.F.B.J. (Société Française de Fabrication des Bébés et Jouets), which is better known for manufacturing dolls. These figures were made of plaster composition, much the same material that dolls were made of. In 1984, when they were sold at Phillips, their origin was unknown, and 52 were sold for £340 (**f**). In 1986, eight figures in an attributed box, although in worse condition, sold for £180 (**H**). *Phillips*

for the composition material), and by Lineol. There were also a number of other firms in Germany, Austria, Belgium and Italy operating on similar principles, Durso of Belgium being a good example.

Elastolin and Lineol toys were widely distributed during the 1920s, and the companies manufactured a variety of models of foreign armies, including Household Cavalry, Foot Guards, Highlanders, lancers, line infantry and World War I fighting troops of the British Army. The most common scale used approximated 70mm, but 60mm, 55mm and 100mm scale figures can also be found. The 55mm figures may have been meant to compete with Britains' output, but they are not nearly so attractive as the larger figures and are not much sought after by collectors.

In the 1930s Elastolin and Lineol were caught up in the rise of the Nazi party and the resurgence of German nationalism, and both companies produced and distributed an enormous variety of German Army, Nazi party and personality figures. To go with these were tinplate vehicles and guns with intricate working parts, electric lights and clockwork motors in the best traditions of the German toy making industry.

The two firms were so fiercely competitive that virtually everything made by the one was mirrored by the other, and Neil Crowley has put together an extremely interesting display, which demonstrates this characteristic of late 1930s manufacture.

Elastolin continued after World War II, but it no longer produced

This group of tinplate 70mm scale vehicles from the Hanington collection includes items by Elastolin and Lineol and some by Tippco. These were made about 1938 to accompany the composition figures of the German Army. Some of the vehicles are in field grey, some in camouflage, and most have clockwork motors (**G–K**). *Phillips*

German Army figures and switched to the manufacture of plastic figures after 1958. Many of the servicemen who took part in the Allied invasion of Germany in 1945 and many of those who later served in Germany, acquired as souvenirs examples of the Nazi and German Army figures, and so started an interest in collecting them that has remained strong in Britain and the United States ever since. Both Elastolin and Lineol produced extensive catalogues, which are now available in reprint, and it is partly for this reason that, after Britains, the toy soldiers produced by these companies are probably the most widely collected.

Composition figures are distinctively wooden in appearance and seem as if hand-carved. Usually they are meticulously painted. Their attraction as toys, particularly in the larger scales, is very considerable, and the tinplate vehicles and wooden buildings are delightful. Today there is a lively market for these items in Germany as well as in Britain and the United States, and there are a number of German dealers.

ALUMINIUM TOY SOLDIERS

After World War II, toy makers became intrigued by the possibilities of a new metal that was coming into common use: aluminium. French manufacturers developed a technique of casting in fine sand, the leading firm being Quiralu. Mignot also tried the process under the tradename Mignalu. As usual with French manufacturers, French subjects formed almost all of the output, although a few of the more famous foreign troops, such as the Papal State Swiss Guard and West Point Cadets, have been

OPPOSITE ABOVE AND ABOVE
Seen here are some of the enormous variety of poses of the German Army and S.A. produced by Elastolin. Lineol manufactured a similar range, but the bases were square rather than round. Both companies usually added their trademarks underneath the figures (**g-j**). *Phillips*

OPPOSITE BELOW
These tinplate Lineol vehicles in 70mm scale were made to accompany the German Army troops (J). The motorcycle combination carries a demountable machine gun, although the gunner is missing (**F**). *Phillips*

found. Not many Napoleonic First Empire troops were forthcoming, as the aluminium casting process did not lend itself to fine detail. The large ranges were in French modern infantry of the 1940s and 1950s and in North African colonial figures, many with the most splendidly colourful uniforms.

The possibilities of aluminium were tried out in England by a firm called Wend-Al, which borrowed the French technology and some French designs and painters to start up in Dorset. For a short time Wend-Al's "unbreakable" figures were quite widely distributed in Britain, and at first painting standards were high, but the advent of the cheaper, moulded plastic toy soldier with a similar "unbreakable" selling claim drove Wend-Al out of the market.

Aluminium figures are beginning to be collected in France, but in Britain there is little interest and they remain cheap. The casting process precludes the fine detail that is possible with other methods and materials, and so the figures tend to look crude and "blobby" beside other toy soldiers. Aluminium is a light and distinctive metal, so identification is simple, and the figures give off a musical clink when knocked lightly against each other.

A troop of paper hussars designed by Richard Simkin and sold in a box devised to resemble two cavalry pillbox hats when the two halves are taken apart. About 45mm scale, these figures are set up as a display sample, which can be folded in four on the "pop-up" principle. The soldiers have pins for swords (**F**). *Author's collection*

DIE-CAST TOY SOLDIERS

Britain was the birthplace of the die-cast toy car in the form of the Dinky Toy, and it was perhaps inevitable that this process should be tested for toy soldiers. Britains started to use zinc alloy casting machinery for making such items as wheels after World War II, and the company made a mould for eight figures in the second-grade range, which were then produced in large quantities for little cost. These figures were preceded by the personnel made by Meccano for its Dinky Toy army vehicles, although only a small range of these 25mm figures was produced.

These early figures proved to be the forerunners of a more interesting series by Britains, which started in 1973 with a Scots Guard. From 1982 onwards, Britains has used die-casting to re-introduce into its catalogue a metal toy soldier range, which is aimed at both the collector and the souvenir markets.

The advantage of the die-casting process is that, once the expensive original dies are made, very large quantities of precision castings can be quickly produced at low cost, as opposed to the solid-cast and hollow-cast methods. Britains has also been experimenting with semi-automatic painting techniques, with the result that a good-looking metal figure can

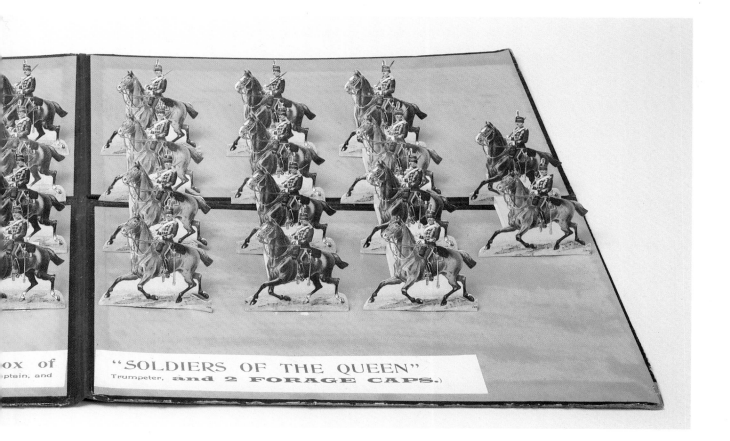

"SOLDIERS OF THE QUEEN"

ox of ptain, and   Trumpeter, and 2 FORAGE CAPS.)

be put on the market for about a third of the cost of the solid-cast figures produced for the collector by other methods. The only brake on further variety is the capital cost of the dies themselves, and expansion has been relatively slow. Nevertheless, the figures produced so far are good to look at and have been widely appreciated and collected.

PAPER TOY SOLDIERS

Since early times printers have run off sheets of paper with rows of soldiers illustrated on them so that they can be cut out, coloured and stood up as toys. Cut-out toy soldiers have continued to be popular, particularly in France and Germany. Epinal Prints are probably the most famous of the names associated with paper toy soldiers, but the coloured sheets that they produced are so decorative it seems a shame to cut them up, even though they are being reproduced today.

The problem with paper soldiers is that they tend to be light and fragile, and, of course, because they are just as flat as flat tin soldiers, they do not fit into displays of round figures. Collectors tend to concentrate on the sheets themselves, of which there are an enormous variety, and some are extremely rare and valuable. However, this is an almost totally separate collecting field from the hollow-cast toy soldier.

Other paper toy soldiers include those made of scraps, cut-out cards, soldiers to go with cut-out toy forts, coronation souvenir cut-outs and press-out cigarette cards. A Gamage's catalogue for 1906 advertised a cardboard "pillbox" soldier hat full of soldiers with swords of the finest steel – these turned out to be ordinary dressmaking pins, inserted into the hands of cardboard cut-out cavalry. I also remember the great excitement of cutting out cardboard figures of the 1953 coronation procession from the backs of Shredded Wheat packets.

DIME-STORE FIGURES

A book on collecting toy soldiers would not be complete without a mention of the dime-store figure. The "five and dime store", selling items at 5 or 10 cents in the United States of America during the 1930s, was the favoured outlet for distributing single toy soldiers and the favourite shop for a visit by a boy with a coin to spend. The best buy for a dime was one of the 70mm chunky-looking hollow-cast models manufactured by Barclay or Manoil, although some of the figures made during the war years were of composition or rubber. This very distinctive genre of toy soldier has become known as the dime-store figure.

Fuelled by the nostalgia of men who grew up in that era, a whole market has sprung up of collectors who want nothing but these and related items from the same source. Very few of these figures ever find their way, or are collected, outside the United States, but for those who like them, there are specialist dealers and sufficient literature on which to base a collection. To demonstrate how sought after these figures are, a rare example of a single figure was recently on offer for $1,200.

PLASTIC TOY SOLDIERS

The world of toys, including toy soldiers, was revolutionized by the invention of plastic moulding materials, which made possible the manufacture of much cheaper mass-produced parts in more intricate shapes than ever before. Plastic materials have now become available with all sorts of strengths and properties, but at first not all plastics were entirely satisfactory, and indeed it is still true that the more flexible and thus less fragile types do not hold paint very well. I have possessed toys made of a sort of crumbly Bakelite, which may class as the earliest sort of plastic, but the first commercial attempt to manufacture plastic toy soldiers in Britain was set up in Dover in 1947 by Malleable Mouldings, which used Holgar Eriksson designs very similar to Authenticast. These figures cannot have been widely distributed, since they are now very rare, and indeed, they were made of such fragile plastic that bayonets or rifles often snapped off very easily.

The first commercially successful plastic toy soldier company was Herald Miniatures, which started production in 1953 and soon became associated with, and later was bought by, Britains. From 1954 onward Herald toy soldiers and those produced by many competitors were made of a flexible plastic that, in its pure form, was virtually unbreakable. Since the use of lead alloys for toy making was at this time beginning to be frowned upon as being potentially harmful to children, a combined sales message of "safe and unbreakable" provided two telling advantages in the

These plastic English Civil War figures by Herald are considered to be among the best ever made by that company. There are only four foot (f) and two mounted (i) poses, but they were produced in a number of different painting styles. Since the pikemen and musketeers of both sides looked similar, a large encounter as shown here looks quite realistic, especially as the toys are so beautifully sculpted. The Rose military miniature musketeer with his musket over his shoulder (centre right) does not look out of place (f). *Author's collection*

toy market for the plastic toy soldier, although naturally they did not carry much weight with adult collectors at the time.

Many of the existing toy soldier manufacturers moved with the times and started to manufacture plastic toy soldiers alongside their existing ranges, and it was clear within a year or two which were the more popular. Once the investment in plastic injection moulding machinery had been made, plastic figures were also much cheaper to make than metal ones, although they still had to be painted by hand. Existing British toy soldier manufacturers that turned to plastic included Timpo, Crescent, Cherilea and Charbens. Hill tried to make the transition but, after producing about half a dozen ranges, gave up the struggle and went into liquidation in 1958. New firms that started out with plastic toy soldiers included Lone Star, Kentoy, Trojan and Speedwell. Of the newcomers, only Lone Star established itself as a major manufacturer, and, with Timpo, Crescent, Cherilea, Charbens and Herald, reigned supreme in the plastic toy soldier market in Britain from 1955 to 1963.

In Europe too, plastic figures came on the market. The principal manufacturers were Elastolin in Germany, which simply continued its traditions of meticulous design and paintwork (which were, if anything, better in the new material) and Starlux in France, whose output, particularly its medieval and ancient portrayals, was, in its own way, just as attractive. In the United States, Louis Marx started producing play sets

Sonnenburg of Germany constructed this toy gun team and gunners of the Royal Horse Artillery of plaster and wood. The uniforms suggest the Crimean War, which dates the toy to 1860–70. The paintwork has been beautifully executed, as befits an expensive toy, and the horses are mounted on springs to simulate movement. This set, which is somewhat damaged, nevertheless realized £3,500 at Phillips in 1987 (**M**). *Phillips*

of unpainted plastic figures with tinplate and plastic accessories, and it was this type of toy soldier that eventually unseated the British hand-painted plastic figure from its pre-eminence in Britain.

Perhaps because it had been necessary to paint the bare lead alloy toy soldiers to make them safe as toys, toy soldier makers in Britain did not at first realize that it was perfectly possible to issue unpainted plastic figures that could be painted by the children themselves. Plastic had also brought to the toy market the polystyrene plastic model kit, and it was Airfix, the premier manufacturer of these kits, which first marketed unpainted toy soldiers in Britain. At first these were available in packets of 20mm scale figures suitable for use with plastic kit vehicles in a similar scale, and they caused an upsurge of interest in war-gaming, since a box of 44 figures cost two shillings (10p). Somewhat later, Airfix started to bring out 54mm figures, and this sounded the death knell for the manufacturers of hand-painted figures. Even though various novelties, such as figures with movable parts (Swoppets) or figures with different coloured plastic parts automatically assembled by machine and so forth were manufactured, children still tended to prefer to buy maybe six uncoloured figures for the price of one coloured one, and this, combined with a flood of imported competition from Hong Kong, where labour costs were lower, eventually drove all the earlier manufacturers except Britains out of business by 1981.

Other companies such as Matchbox in Britain and Atlantic in Italy started to produce uncoloured plastic troops in large scale, and today this sort of figure is almost all that one can buy in toyshops. Even the figures from Hong Kong are mostly unpainted. Britains still produces a limited range of "Deetail" figures, which have metal bases, but the far greater part of the company's production is in civilian die-cast vehicles. The picture is much the same elsewhere, with only Starlux in France producing any large range. Elastolin came to an end in Germany, although there are signs of a successor company, and no major manufacturer of painted plastic figures exists in Italy, Spain or the United States.

During the period 1947 to 1980, toy soldiers, thanks to plastic and worldwide distribution, had become more widespread than ever before, and were probably produced in greater variety, certainly in many more countries, than previously. Boys who were introduced to toy soldiers with plastic figures were usually born in 1950 or later, so the plastic generation is now growing up, and the nostalgic pull of the older plastic models is exerting much the same fascination that the metal ones had for earlier generations, and plastic figures now have quite a following among collectors. There are just as many production rarities among the plastics as with any other sort of toy soldier, and, because they tended (being "unbreakable") to be treated much less kindly than the metal ones, possibly fewer will actually survive. Plastic figures have still not become as expensive to collect as metal ones, but they are nevertheless already featuring in auctions.

UNUSUAL TOY SOLDIERS

Although the vast majority of toy soldiers have been made by the methods already outlined in this chapter, the urge to produce military miniatures as toys has not been limited to these alone. I have always rather liked to have an example of all the different sorts of toy soldiers that have been made, and this interest is, I know, shared by many other collectors. The late John G. Garratt made it a life's ambition to learn about all the toy *and* model figures ever made, and in his *World Encyclopedia of Model Soldiers* he listed many hundreds of manufacturers and dozens of different manufacturing processes. In my own collection I have plaster figures from China and India, foam rubber troops from Italy and soldiers made out of soap, papier mâché, lithographed tin, jointed tinplate, wood and china. Toy makers needing soldiers to add to toy games and curiosities have often made them themselves in ingenious fashion from whatever material has been to hand. The French doll manufacturing company, Société Française de Fabrication des Bébés et Jouets (S.F.B.J.), made toy soldiers of French infantry in 100mm scale from a material akin to the bisque used for dolls' heads.

To collect from so wide a range of toy figures is quite an adventure, but if the whole range of options of what may be collected is not there to choose from, can it truly be said that the collecting speciality that is selected is right?

3
COLLECTING TOY SOLDIERS TODAY

Toy soldiers have always been collectable items for children, because the more soldiers they have, the more fun they can have with them. As well as professional soldiers, who use such toys for war-gaming and parade planning, there have always been enlightened adults – such as H.G. Wells – who, understanding the value of continued fun throughout life, went on collecting and playing regardless of their age.

Until 1960 collecting toy soldiers posed no real problems. Supplies were relatively plentiful in the toyshops, and it was possible to go out and buy what one wanted. The members of the British Model Soldier Society (B.M.S.S.), which was founded in 1935, were more concerned with converting toy soldiers into realistic models, which was cheaper and/or less trouble than making a model from scratch or buying a real figurine.

Even at this time there were a number of adults collecting discontinued toy soldiers, notably Len Richards and Edmund Roche Kelly. From 1960 until 1966 it was still possible to buy Britains hollow-cast figures in the toyshops, but all other British manufacturers had turned to plastic production. Shamus Wade was at this period selling from a stall in the Portobello Road, London, and Len Richards brought collections for sale through the B.M.S.S. along to the meetings at the Caxton Hall. Individual Britains figures were on sale at Hamleys in London for about 1s 6d (7 new pence) and a rare discontinued figure from Shamus Wade might cost twice that. I was in my magpie collecting phase, but as a schoolboy I had few funds and preferred his broken figures at one penny each.

Once Britains ceased the production of hollow-cast figures in 1966, it became apparent that many collectors were forced into the second-hand market, and there was a flurry of activity as people rushed around toyshops to buy up old stock. I acquired a *set 73* in this way on my twenty-first birthday. Disposal of collections at the B.M.S.S. became a frenetic affair, the prices still being low but the demand high and the supply insufficient. Members took turns by throwing dice for the privilege of being the first to choose an item from a collection on sale. Len Richards was forming a core of Britains collectors by his activities, and he also allowed a few of the keenest members to visit his home, where he had 18,000 figures in his attic (a space about 10 feet square). My own first visit there was marked by the purchase for the sum of £1 2s 6d (£1.12) of a boxed monoplane, an item I still treasure. At the time he had six of them to sell from a collection he was breaking up.

Listening to him describe the intimate detail of the changes in version from valise pack to box pack in Britains 1905 infantry, inspired me to all my later academic endeavours. At the time I was collecting new issues of plastic figures as they came out, since plastic figures were what I could afford. Len Richards, on hearing this, presented me with some 500 early plastic items, on the condition that I classified them and wrote them up, as he was doing for metal figures. Even though I have since tried to improve on his own work in the B.M.S.S. bulletin and in his book (published in 1970), I hope I have repaid his investment.

Within 10 years of Britains ceasing production in 1966, two major developments took place that effectively shaped the modern toy soldier collecting environment.

A miscellany of soldiers. Top row: the first six figures from the left are French-made hollow-cast figures (**e**); next are four figures, also French, made in aluminium by Quiralu to depict Algerian tribal infantry (**e**); on the right is a group of semi-flat die-cast Soviet infantry made in the U.S.S.R. (**c**).

All the figures in the middle row are from the United States: the horse is by Warren; the next figure, of unknown make, depicts the 7th New York Volunteers (**f**); the next two figures are also of unknown make; the kneeling, firing federal infantryman is a Bussler (**d**); and the

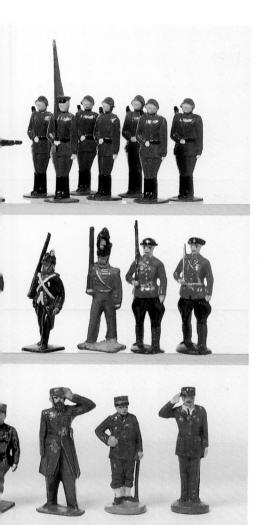

American War of Independence Highlander is a Scheid (**e**). The figure fourth from right is marked *Lincoln Logs* (**d**), but the others (**c**) remain a mystery.

On the bottom row the two mounted figures are French hollow-cast depictions of the Emperor Haile Selassie of Ethiopia (**h**) and Napoleon I (**e**); then comes a Starlux plastic eagle bearer of the Imperial Guard (**c**), and a group of French officers (**e**), all but the two on the right being hollow-cast, the other aluminium. Some appear to be personality figures. *Author's collection*

First, it occurred to an auctioneer named Richard Lane that toy soldiers could become the subject of a specialist auction, and the first of these was held in 1969 at Knight, Frank & Rutley. Richard Lane joined Phillips shortly thereafter, and over 80 specialized toy soldier sales have been held by that establishment in London and New York with approximately a million and a half figures marching under the hammer. To put that figure into perspective: Britains original production was at one stage running at half a million castings a week! Once auctions had started, the prices to be paid or received for second-hand toy soldiers became much better known, and several more dealers became established with worldwide postal sales lists.

By 1972 another idea took root that completed the modern collecting scene. Jan and Frank Scroby, who were selling old toy soldiers from a stall in the Portobello Road, decided that supplies were so short that it would be profitable to make new ones specifically for the collector market. Peter Cowan wanted to fill out the ranks of Britains figures with similar items that Britains never made. Jan and Frank's idea became Blenheim Models, and Peter's was first marketed as Gunner but soon after became Mark Time. It was an idea whose time had come, for the advent of small, vulcanized rubber, centrifugal casting machinery at a reasonable price meant that new figures could be cast and painted for half the current price of a second-hand toy. Over the next 14 years, at least 50 manufacturers or series were started along similar lines although with varying degrees of success.

The next logical development was more literature on the subject, and in 1977 the *Old Toy Soldier Newsletter* was started in Illinois, U.S.A., followed by *Toy Soldier Review* on the East Coast in 1984. Various people, including myself, issued listings of catalogue numbers and information, followed by books (see Bibliography, page 140). All this activity has as its object to make the subject of toy soldiers more intriguing and satisfying to the enquiring mind.

SEARCHING FOR TOY SOLDIERS

Hunting for toy soldiers is difficult, because the hobby is not fully mature and there are not enough people collecting for it to be worthwhile to cater for them extensively. Thinking of the facilities enjoyed by stamp or coin collectors can make a toy soldier collector feel decidedly underprivileged, but then the toy soldier collector is a much more unusual individual and must make the most of his advantages.

It is still possible to find toy soldiers in the possession of friends or relatives who are only too happy to donate them to a good cause, and this has formed the nucleus of many a collection. Make your interest known to as many people as possible. It is sometimes rewarding to advertise in local papers, and I know of several collectors who have made very good discoveries using this means. One must be prepared for disappointments as well, and the watchword is perseverance, which probably means laying out quite large sums on advertising in personal columns.

Britains Hunting Series (**e**–**g**) and, in the foreground, a rare Britains motorbicycle and sidecar (**l**). *Phillips*

BELOW
A selection of interesting German and British figures made from 1900 to 1910. Identifying the manufacturers of all these figures is difficult, but the sixth figure from the left on the top row is a Japanese-made copy of a Heyde figure, produced by a firm called Minikin about 1950. The third and fourth figures from the left on the top row are by Reka. The rest are of uncertain origin, although many are solid figures by Heyde (**e**). *Author's collection*

Real searching starts in hunting round junk shops and antique shops. Perhaps there are not very many of the real junk shops left today – they have been replaced by charity shops, car boot sales and jumble sales. By spending a great deal of time attending these and searching in the inevitable box of second-hand toys, it is possible to come up with various things, although in my experience it will not be often.

More promising are the antique and curiosity shops, many of which like to sell old toys when they can get them. Leaving a name and address with as many as one can reach can pay dividends. Antique and collectors fairs also sometimes produce items. The proportion of toy soldiers to be found in the general antique trade, however, is very small compared to the specialized toy collecting fairs, usually known as swapmeets, one or two of which now are usually held every weekend in every region of Britain and the United States, so much so that attending them is a way of life for an increasing number of dealers. Most of the people at these events who take tables to sell things have their own collecting speciality, be it boats, trains or Dinky Toys, but the toy theme is common to all, and each will gather in all the toys within reach to take to the swapmeets in order to sell them and buy the things that they specialize in instead. Thus, whatever the stall, there is always a good possibility of a scattering of toy soldiers, although their owner's idea of a correct price to ask for them may be different from yours.

Among the swapmeet dealers are some who incline towards toy soldiers, and there are a scattering of real toy soldier shops, particularly in London. Some of the shops that sell a more general line of collectable toys also feature toy soldiers among their offerings, so it is worth going to these on the same principle as going to swapmeets. The publication *Collectors Gazette* gives details of swapmeets and contains the advertisements of the shops; it is on sale at most swapmeets. *Exchange and Mart* also contains details of swapmeets and sometimes of toys for sale.

Finally, there are the real specialists, the dealers and shops whose main livelihood is with toy soldiers. There are not many, but most advertise in the *Old Toy Soldier Newsletter*, the *Toy Soldier Review*, *Plastic Warrior*, the *Bulletin of the British Model Soldier Society* and *Military Modelling*, which are the five publications catering to toy soldier collectors, though the latter two are for modellers as well (see Bibliography).

In addition, there are the auctioneers, among which Phillips in London and New York is the only one to have sales devoted entirely to toy soldiers. Probably some 200,000 toy soldiers are marched through the auction rooms each year, so it is well worth paying them a visit. Local auctions are also worth attending, particularly if there are a number of lots of toy soldiers, but occasionally enthusiastic rather than knowledgeable local bidders will push the price higher than one would expect to pay in London or New York.

The highlights of the collecting year are the major meetings of collectors and specialists. These are the equivalent of swapmeets but organized exclusively for toy and model soldiers. In Britain, the British Model Soldier Society has regular national meetings attended by dealers, as well as the Annual Modelmaking Competitions, regional open days and private auctions. In the United States, the *Old Toy Soldier Newsletter* annual show in Chicago has two hundred tables devoted to toy soldiers, with other leading shows being the Chester show and the East Coast show.

AUCTION HINTS FOR THE BEGINNER

The auction room is a very new environment for those who are not accustomed to it, but many collectors who are inhibited from attending miss their chance of acquiring good value items. Newcomers should remember the following points:

1. Examine everything carefully during the viewing hours to make sure it is as described. You are buying the items themselves, not the auctioneer's description. There is no substitute for going to view an auction: until you have seen a lot, you can have no way of assessing its personal value to you. For the finer points of condition, see pages 60–8.

2. Decide for yourself what you are prepared to pay for the lot. If the estimate shown seems low, expect the bidding to go higher. If the item particularly fits your collection, it may be worth more to you than to other people.

3. Do not be put off by the comments of those around you. Some people attend the viewing with the intention of passing derogatory opinions in a loud voice – it helps to keep the price down for them.

4. Sit where you can comfortably hear and be seen by the auctioneer. Some bidders cluster at the back because they want to see who else is bidding.

5. If the general level of prices on the first lots of the sale seems exorbitant, decide quickly if the general level of prices has gone up. If so, are you prepared to go higher than intended in order to get what you want?

6. The auction will proceed at a brisk pace, maybe 200 lots an hour, one lot every 20 seconds. Be prepared to bid when your lot comes, and make yourself known to the auctioneer by a strong, decisive wave of your hand or paddle. If you cannot catch his eye at first, it will be because he is attending to two other bidders, but when one of them drops out, he will look around for further bids; if you are still interested, you will then be able to attract his attention.

7. Expect the bidding to go up by about 10 per cent of the price of the previous bid – i.e., £10 – 12 – 15 – 18 – 20 – 22 – 25 – 28 – 30 to £50; then £55 – 60 – 65 – 70 to £100; then £110 – 120 – 130 – to £200, then £220 and so on.

8. Remember that often a seller's premium plus V.A.T. – usually at a total of 11½ per cent – is added to the hammer price, which means

that on a bid of £65, the actual price you pay is £72.48. Adjust your high limit accordingly.

9. Try not to get carried away by competing with another bidder up to a price that is higher than you really wanted to pay, unless you have already prepared for this under point 5 above.

10. Do not be tempted to bid for something that seems to be going cheap but that you did not look at before the sale. Odds on, there is a reason for the low price.

11. Do not bid for a mixed lot to get one item in it, hoping that the value of the rest of the lot can be recouped by resale. If the item you want is worth the whole price to you, fair enough – you got the rest for nothing – but feeling that you have been forced to buy things you do not want in large lots is not pleasant. See if you can acquire these single pieces from dealers.

12. If, when you examine what you have bought, it seems to be not as you saw it on view before the auction, complain. A reputable auctioneer will make a part or full refund if your complaint is reasonable.

13. Do not expect the auctioneer to provide proper packing material – bring your own (see Chapter 10).

14. If you want to bid on many items, but have an overall budget to spend, keep a running total after purchasing each lot.

15. The lot is sold on the auctioneer bringing down his hammer. If two people sitting very near to each other are bidding, it may not be immediately clear who was successful. If in doubt, shout out "Was that mine?", and if there was a genuine muddle, the auctioneer may restart the bidding. In all these matters, the auctioneer's decision is final, but he will be trying to please.

16. If the level of prices is up, and you have decided you could afford to spend a certain sum spread between a fixed list of lots, add the unsuccessful bid price to your next lot to be bid, and keep a running total of what you have in hand. For example:
Bid 1 Go to £50 – unsuccessful – carry forward £50.
Bid 2 Go to £80 – add £50 – successful at £120 – carry forward £10.
Bid 3 Go to £30 – add £10 – unsuccessful – carry forward £40.
Bid 4 Go to £60 – add £40 – unsuccessful – carry forward £100.
Bid 5 Go to £80 – add £100 – successful at £130 – carry forward £50.
This roll-up method virtually assures success at some point, and in a rising market will overcome the fright of paying too much for one item while keeping within the bounds of an overall budget.

REFERENCE MATERIAL

For straightforward books on toy soldiers, the reader is referred to the Bibliography on page 140. However, collectors will probably want to have more to refer to than these. It is helpful to have as many catalogues of toy soldiers as possible (see pages 84–7) and books on uniforms of the world's armed forces can sometimes be helpful in identifying an unusual figure and be of good service when making up a particular thematic collection

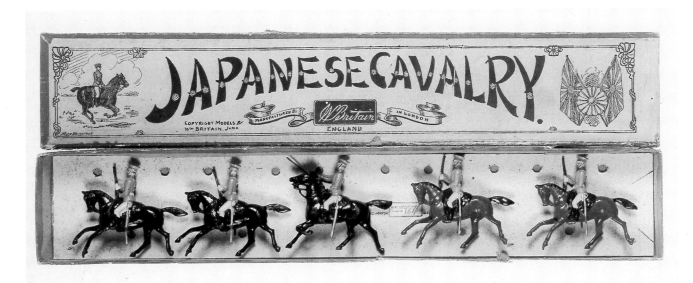

Britains *set 135*, Japanese Cavalry, with a box illustrated by Whisstock (l, j). *Phillips*

with converted figures (see Chapter 8). Many collectors also enjoy reading military history.

Apart from this there is very little reference material available. All the most important knowledge that is not in the few reference books will come from articles in the magazines given in the Bibliography or from conversations with other collectors. These conversations are what make the society meetings and shows so worthwhile.

There is, however, no substitute for viewing as many toy soldiers as possible. During your searches for toy soldiers to acquire, the actual looking at ones that are not wanted can be as important as buying the ones that are.

It is a shame that there are not more public museum exhibitions of toy soldiers on permanent display, but they do not yet merit the important position taken by art or antiquities. Most toy museums have a certain number of toy soldiers on view, the Bethnal Green Museum of Childhood in London having a particularly good display, but the most comprehensive collection in the world is probably the Forbes collection, comprising over 70,000 figures, which is housed in the Palais Mendoub, Tangier, Morocco, and this is on view to visitors.

4
PAINTWORK AND UNIFORMS

RECOGNIZING MANUFACTURERS' STYLES

Every manufacturer of toy soldiers has an individual style, which is usually recognizable once you have seen enough examples of that manufacturer's work. The things that go to make up the style are the recognition marks (if any), the sculpturing of the figures, the style of the paintwork and the material from which the soldiers are made. Normally, if a group of one manufacturer's figures is displayed together, it will have a definite harmony and will contrast with the figures of any other manufacturer that are set among it. Once again, experience of handling large numbers of toy soldiers will enable you to recognize a manufacturer's style, and it is more obvious with some manufacturers than others. I, for instance, who specialize in British hollow-cast figures, do not have much feeling for the differences between flat figures or German solid-cast figures of similar types.

When you look at a figure, the first step is to search to see if there are any letters or symbols anywhere on the casting. The favourite place for these is under the base on which the figure stands or, on cavalry figures, under the horse's belly. Sometimes, however, marks appear down a trouser leg, in the decoration of a saddle-cloth or across a figure's shoulders. Often, all that is in evidence is an unhelpful "Made in England", but even this can be a good clue if the lettering style used is of a consistent sort, as with Timpo or Charbens. After 1900, Britains invariably identified its figures, and other makers that normally named their products on the figures were Hill, Cherilea, Timpo, Charbens, Elastolin, Lineol, Lone Star, Marx and Starlux. Many others did so intermittently, particularly if they were figures of which they were especially proud.

Recognizing the sculpturing of figures is very much a question of having an eye for it, although certain features may be seen to be common to different figures. If a figure has movable arms, for instance, the same arm on an unidentified figure as on one already known will be enough for identification purposes. Most manufacturers had a consistent style for their figures but with peculiarities, such as a small but constant variation in scale – B.M.C. figures, for example, were either a little larger than Britains (58mm) or a little smaller (52mm). Other manufacturers, on the other hand, were very inconsistent, notably Crescent, Reka, Hanks, Hill and Fry. Sometimes, as with Cherilea and Timpo, three or more distinct

Britains specials – a 1st Dragoon at the halt and an officer of the 4th Dragoon Guards (j). *Phillips*

BELOW
Britains invited customers to ask for special
models or paintings to their requirements,
and many such figures were produced
during the 1930s. The standard of painting
could be similar to the normal toys, or
carried out more expensively with
additional detail. Since many people had
connections with the Indian Army, India
being part of the British Empire at the time,
special paintings were often commissioned
using the Indian Army regiments as subjects.
This group of cavalry is the largest single
group of special paint figures known to me
(**M, k**). It depicts a Madras Lancer Regiment
with an Indian officer and a British officer
painted from a 17th Lancer casting. This
group does not have any additional paint
detail. *Phillips*

RIGHT
The two infantry on the left are men from
Britains *set 67*, the 1st Madras Native
Infantry. The cavalryman is an extremely
rare figure (**k**), probably from *set 2013*,
which was issued for a short time in 1948,
possibly to celebrate the independence of
India. The next two infantry are special
paintings with extra detail (**j**), and the figure
on the right is from *set 1621*, the 12th
Frontier Force (**i**). *Phillips*

styles were used over the years of production, and this is a great help in recognizing when the soldiers were made. The shape of the base can also be helpful, as this tended to be similar throughout any given series from one manufacturer.

Paintwork is primarily a matter of the number of colours used and the care with which they are applied. Some firms produced figures with three or more grades of paintwork, since the painting was a very large component of the cost of manufacture. German and French toy soldiers have nearly always been beautifully painted in the best toy making traditions, which is one reason why they are so attractive. Britains figures were painted in a standard best quality, a second grade of up to five colours, a cheap quality of three colours and sometimes just in gold paint. Some other British manufacturers tried to emulate Britains best quality, which included collar and cuff colours, gold buttons, eyes, cheeks and mouths or moustaches, but most found it easier to compete in the second grade or cheapest markets. B.M.C. is notable for the high quality of its paintwork, as are the better products of Reka, Hill, Renvoize and Timpo. Best quality paintwork is almost invariably more attractive to collect than the cheaper grades.

Another pointer to the manufacturer can be the actual consistency or brightness of the paint, and this is also a good guide to the age of the figure, since paints from 1890 to 1905 tend to be less smooth and less finely ground than later paints and hence look matt. Lead-based paints have a different sheen, with more depth to it, than plastic-based paints, which have more of a surface gloss to them. Different manufacturers used different qualities of paint, different shades of red and blue, and often, consistently, a certain shade of green for the bases. Segal figures, for instance, usually have extremely dark green bases.

The quality of the metal underneath the paint also affected the paint colours, although it is difficult to be dogmatic about this because the surface of the metal could change depending on the length of time between casting and painting. Hanks and Renvoize in particular, however, used a metal that contained more tin and less antimony than other manufacturers, and it gave a harder, brighter look to the bare metal underneath the base. Consistent differences between manufacturers are evident along these lines.

It is perfectly possible to have large numbers of figures by unknown manufacturers already sorted into groups that would all be by the same maker if only it were known who that was. The breakthrough usually comes by way of an illustration in a newly unearthed illustrated catalogue, or by finding some of the figures in an original and identifiable box.

CLUES TO DATING BRITAINS

The production of Britains hollow-cast toy soldiers continued from 1893 until 1966, with a few years cessation during the world wars. Although the appearance of Britains toy soldiers is, overall, distinct from that of all

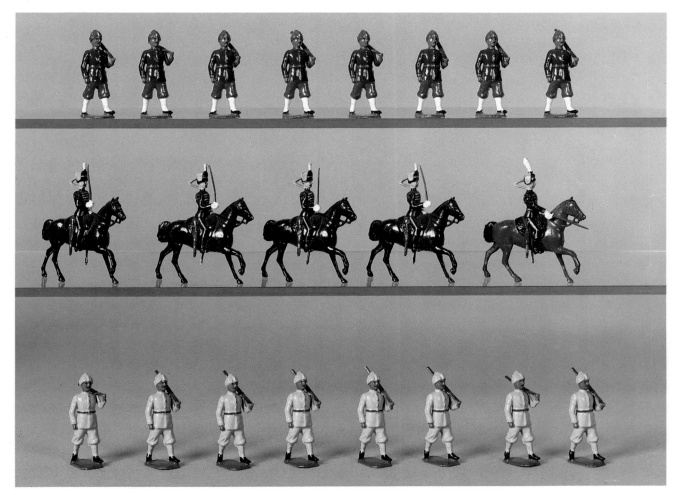

other makers, there are interesting evolutions in the style of the figures and clues to recognition that enable a reasonably close dating to be given to any Britains figure. If a catalogue number is known for the figure, all the years before that catalogue number was brought out can be discounted, since, with few exceptions, the numbering was built up in chronological sequence. Here is a short summary of the dates for catalogue numbers, the highest number given having been produced by the year shown:

1894	24	*1924*	215	*1938*	1658
1896	68	*1927*	252	*1940*	1920
1898	94	*1929*	399	*1948*	2026
1901	126	*1932*	500	*1951*	2060
1906	147	*1934*	1390	*1954*	2097
1911	168	*1936*	1463	*1955*	2117
1916	197	*1937*	1616	*1960*	2189

The top set of these Britains specials is of an Indian Army Rajput Regiment (**I**), and the bottom set is a neat rendition of the Frontier Force (**H**) – compare them with the Indian Army figures illustrated on page 47. The row of cavalry in the centre is a special set of 4th Hussars (**I**). Britains normal representation of the 4th Hussars is in catalogue set *8*, which shows them at the full gallop with a trumpeter. Here is a set based on the horse normally used for the Scots Greys and with an officer. *Phillips*

Remember that numbers 501 to 1200 were not military items and numbers 1921 to 2000 were not used.

The following dates are the approximate times when styles of toy soldier manufacture changed at Britains:

1893 Start of production. Oval bases, fixed arms.
1896 Introduction of the movable arm.
1900 Paper dating labels put on new figures, followed by inscribed dates on bases; bases, previously blank, henceforth marked *Britains*.
1908 Introduction of rectangular ("square") bases.
1914 New figures no longer have dates inscribed.
1924 Existing moulds with dates phased out.
1924 Introduction of light-harness team-horses.
1933 Phasing out of gaitered figures, replaced by full trousers.
1939 Moustaches cease to be painted on the figure.
1949 Introduction of full colour "Regiments of All Nations" boxes.
1955 Bands fitted with plastic drums.
1961 Introduction of window boxes.
1962 Whole catalogue renumbered.
1966 Production ceases.

By using the above clues in concert with the catalogue numbers, it is possible to obtain a rough date for Britains' figures.

RECOGNIZING BRITISH ARMY UNIFORMS

There are several comprehensive books on the market that identify the uniforms of every regiment in the British Army. Toy soldiers, however, were painted in a much simpler fashion. The most commonly found uniform on British hollow-cast toy soldiers is the full dress of the 1890s and 1900s, and Britains best quality paint set the standard for uniforms. On cavalry figures the painted details included collar and cuff facings (unless gauntlets were worn), plume colours or busby bag for hussars and the coloured stripe down the trouser. On infantry figures, the plume was painted on Foot Guards only, but other figures had collar and cuff facings, belt and straps if equipment was worn and the stripe down the trouser. Some other manufacturers also added this amount of detail, but the cheaper the grade, the less detail was applied – by Britains as well as the rest.

Of Britains figures, the Household Cavalry, Dragoons and Dragoon Guards all wore the same cavalry helmet; the Scots Greys, distinctive as the only cavalry regiment with a bearskin cap, looked like mounted Foot Guards. Britains Household Cavalry, Life Guards and Horse Guards had breast- and back-plates, a last vestige of armour, with white breeches and black horses, but the Life Guards had red coats and white plumes and the Horse Guards blue coats and red plumes. Some other makers sometimes mounted cavalry with breastplates on brown horses, thus causing doubt as to whether they were meant to represent Household Cavalry or Dragoon Guards. Among Britains figures the only Dragoon regiment in

OPPOSITE
In the late 1930s many beautiful groups such as this Band of the Royal Fusiliers were commissioned from Britains by L. Poitier-Smith. When his collection was first auctioned at Phillips in 1973, this group fetched £52, which was a high price for that time. When it re-appeared at Phillips in 1985, it fetched £800 (**L**). *Phillips*

Britains special paintings of Indian infantry – the neatness of the paintwork shows up to advantage in close-up (**j**). *Sotheby's*

Britains set *127*, the 4th/7th Dragoon Guards, in its original box. This is one of the very attractive box labels produced for individual sets after Fred Whisstock had stopped designing them (**H, i**). The name of the set was changed from the 7th Dragoon Guards to the 4th/7th Dragoon Guards some time after the amalgamation of the Regiments in the British Army List of 1922. *Phillips*

OPPOSITE ABOVE
This illustration of Britains cavalry of the British Army shows the uniform details used by Britains in its portrayal of cavalry. From top to bottom, left to right, in order of seniority, the regiments are: 1st Life Guards (second grade); 2nd Life Guards; Horse Guards (second grade); 1st King's Dragoon Guards; 2nd Dragoon Guards; 5th Dragoon Guards; 6th Dragoon Guards; 7th Dragoon Guards; 2nd Dragoons Royal Scots Greys; 1st Dragoons (second grade); 3rd Hussars; 4th Hussars; 6th Dragoons; 9th Lancers; 10th Hussars; 11th Hussars; 12th Lancers; 13th Hussars; 16th Lancers; 17th Lancers and 21st Lancers (**i**). *Author's collection*

OPPOSITE BELOW
Britains specials – two figures from a peak cap drum and fife band, two from a different peak cap military band (**J**), and the officer and man from the regular set *2087*, the 5th Dragoon Guards, dismounted at attention (**g**). *Phillips*

full dress, apart from the Scots Greys, was the 1st Dragoons, of which the soldiers were modelled with a silver helmet with a black plume falling straight down the back of it, a red coat and blue breeches with a yellow stripe.

All full-dress Dragoon Guards had bronze-painted helmets – except when Britains painters sometimes wrongly left them silver – and the best means of identifying them is to see how their plumes were coloured. All except the 6th Dragoon Guards had red coats. Red plumes signified the 1st Dragoon Guards, and black plumes, the 2nd Dragoon Guards, which had white or buff facings. The 5th Dragoon Guards had white over red (sometimes vice versa) with green facings, while the 6th Dragoon Guards had white plumes and blue coats. Black over a white plume signified the 7th, or later the 4th/7th, Dragoon Guards.

Hussars may be told apart by the colour of their busby bags. The 3rd Hussars had a blue bag, while the 4th Hussars had a yellow bag. A scarlet bag on horses at the trot signified the 7th Hussars, while a scarlet bag on horses at the halt showed the 10th. The 11th Hussars, nicknamed the "Cherry Pickers", had a crimson busby bag with crimson trousers, and a buff busby bag (sometimes painted white) signified the 13th Hussars. Hussars in a green uniform were the Middlesex Yeomanry. The Royal Horse Artillery looked like hussars, but they would be seen either with gun teams or carrying carbines and with red busby bags.

Lancers had different coloured plumes and plastrons (a plastron being the cloth, in a contrasting colour, across the chest of the tunic). A green plume and red plastron was the 5th Lancers; a black and white plume and red plastron was the 9th Lancers; a red plume and plastron was the 12th Lancers; a black plume and blue plastron on a red coat was the 16th Lancers (later the 16th/5th Lancers); a white plume and plastron was the 17th Lancers; and a white plume and light blue plastron was the 21st

Lancers. Lancer regiments were also apt to be miscoloured by some makers, Crescent even giving some of its figures breastplates.

The Foot Guards are relatively easy to distinguish as they had the massive, furry bearskin caps with the standard British red coats and blue trousers. The five Guards regiments may be differentiated by their plumes: white on the left for the Grenadiers, red on the right for the Coldstreams, no plume at all for the Scots, blue on the right for the Irish and white with a green horizontal stripe on the left for the Welsh. These plumes were usually omitted in cheaper painting grades, but the figures could still legitimately be called Scots Guards. Some of Britains Foot Guards had heads with moulded plumes, which are occasionally on the opposite side of the bearskin from the painted plume, but, as far as I can tell, this has no significance. Britains painters sometimes put the plume on the wrong side, but if it is a red plume, the figure is probably a Canadian Governor General's Foot Guard, on which the plume placing is the only mark that distinguishes it from a Coldstream Guard. The Fusilier regiments wore a raccoon skin cap, which looks like a rather small bearskin cap. Once a few examples have been examined, the difference, with Britains figures, is clear, although Britains never painted plumes on the caps of the Fusiliers, so the regiments cannot be told apart. Other makers sometimes used the same casting for Foot Guards and for Fusiliers.

Highlanders can be distinguished by the stylized painting of their tartans. Britains Black Watch had dark green kilts with black stripes; the Gordons had dark green kilts with yellow stripes; the Seaforth kilts were dark green with red and white stripes; the Argyll and Sutherlands had dark green kilts with light green stripes; and the Camerons had dark blue kilts with red and yellow stripes. Only the Black Watch had a red bonnet hackle; the others had white ones. Lowland regiments wore trews, with either a Kilmarnock bonnet or a shako. The Royal Scots had bonnets with yellow or yellow and red striped trews; and the King's Own Scottish Borderers had bonnets with red and white striped trews. The Highland Light Infantry had shakos with red and white triped trews, while the rare Cameronian Rifles had shakos with white striped trews and an overall uniform of dark green. Makers other than Britains often let their imaginations run riot in the colour of the tartans.

Rifle regiments wore a busby with a short plume at the front and a dark green uniform. The Rifle Brigade plume was black; the King's Royal Rifle Corps had a tuft of red.

Infantry of the Line all wore the spiked infantry helmet, which was blue for most regiments but green for light infantry. Some regiments were shown wearing white foreign-service covers on their helmets. Later, Britains portrayed some infantry in the number one dress with peak caps. Few makers other than Britains issued sets of named regiments of Line Infantry.

Most other makers than Britains produced Household Cavalry, Foot Guards, Highlanders and Infantry of the Line but, apart from that, limited

Here are shown various regiments of the British Army as painted by Britains. From top to bottom, left to right, in order of the Army List of 1914, they are: Grenadier Guards; Coldstream Guards; Scots Guards; Welsh Guards; Irish Guards; Royal Scots; West Surrey; East Kent; Lancaster; Northumberland Fusiliers; Warwickshire; Royal Fusiliers; Devonshire; Somerset Light Infantry; East Yorks; Royal Irish; Green Howards; Lancashire Fusiliers; Royal Welch Fusiliers; Gloucestershire; Worcestershire; Sussex; Black Watch; Middlesex; King's Royal Rifle Corps; Manchester; York and Lancaster; Highland Light Infantry; Seaforth; Gordons; Camerons; Argyll and Sutherland; Dublin Fusiliers and the Rifle Brigade (h).

Author's collection

Britains set *128*, the 12th Lancers, is a companion set to *127* (see page 52), and it uses the same arm with a slung lance. This is an early set with a bold Printers Type box label dating from about 1905 (**G, i**). *Phillips*

Britains sets *24*, the 9th Lancers, are both from the same period, but the box labels have been redone, although the same illustrations have been incorporated into the designs. The label with the smaller titling (above) is the later of the two, since the Regiment's four Boer War battle honours have been added: "South Africa 1899–1902, Modder River, Relief of Kimberley, Paardeberg." These sets show also the alternative ways of displaying a set with its box. The set with the earlier box (below) realized £300 and the other £220 in the same sale in January 1987 (**H, i**). *Phillips*

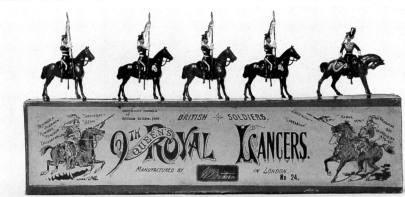

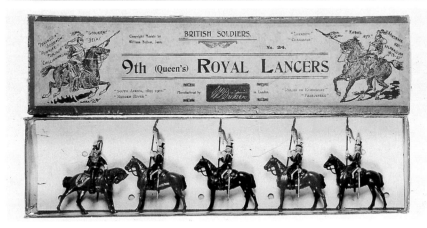

OPPOSITE
These are the labels for *set 72*, first made as a souvenir for Queen Victoria's Diamond Jubilee in 1897. The set was sufficiently popular to be produced later as "Life Guards Past and Present", with a thrifty re-use of most of the earlier label. *Author's collection*

themselves usually to a few regiments of cavalry, Fusiliers, Rifles or Lowlanders, a very narrow range compared with Britains comprehensive output.

The other favourite subject was the British Army in khaki, and here at least it can be told if a model was made before or after 1939 according to whether the uniform portrayed the webbing equipment and puttees of World War I or the battledress with gaiters that was introduced in 1939.

5

PERFECTION AND IMPERFECTION

For many collectors the ultimate ambition is to collect mint toy soldiers in perfect, original boxes, but these are certainly hard to find. Compared with stamps and coins, of which unused or uncirculated perfect specimens are in reasonable supply, toy soldiers tend not to have survived the years in immaculate condition. The quest for perfection can severely stifle the collecting instinct by limiting the number of acquisitions that can be made. It is worth remembering that items first bought in less good state can always be sold again later when better specimens are found. However, some things are so rare that the likelihood of better examples turning up may be extremely remote, and I am often quite satisfied with good condition items in only fair condition boxes. The collection that is entirely perfect is a delight to view but is likely to remain a small one.

COLLECTING SOLDIERS IN ORIGINAL BOXES

The boxes and packaging that the soldiers originally came in are often delightful, not only because of their artistic and stylistic merit, which is often considerable, but also because they re-awaken that feeling of pressing the nose against a toyshop window or of unwrapping a Christmas present, as yet entirely unused and full of potential pleasure. On the next pages are to be found an array of the box labels used by Britains. These show the different styles the company used from the simple, early typeset labels, sometimes with charming wood-cut illustrations, to the more highly decorated, early 20th-century ones, the signed designs of Frederick Whisstock, each with the badge of the regiment, the splendid and intricate designs of the 1930s and the standard but colourful labels of the 1950s. Britains' trademark appeared on each of them before World War II, but other manufacturers were often not so proud of what they had made, and sometimes the packaging gave no better clue than the models to the supplier. Under normal circumstances, however, a name was much more likely to appear on a box than on a figure, as was the case with an interesting lot recently sold at Phillips: the boxes bore the name Locarno Toys, while the contents had previously been on collectors' "unknown" shelves. Collecting boxes, therefore, has also an element of research about it, as boxes often reveal hitherto unknown manufacturers and set numbers.

It is, of course, also true that soldiers in their original boxes are much

OVERLEAF AND PAGE 59
From left to right: Box labels from *sets 133*, Russian Infantry, and *136*, Russian Cavalry; the early title of the boxes was adapted after the Russian Revolution of 1917, but someone at Britains mistook the meaning of the initials U.S.S.R. Various box labels from *sets 69, 75* and *82*, all containing Scots Guards. Boxes for Britains Japanese Infantry and Cavalry that opposed the Russian troops opposite; the Chinese Infantry box labels show that even when a simple design was used, there were multiple changes. A splendid variety of Britains box labels for the Grenadier Guards; sets in the original boxes may be approximately dated from the labels: the top label here was current c.1898–1910; the second 1914–30; the third 1930–40; the fourth, fifth and sixth 1901–20; the seventh 1920–40; and the eighth 1925–55.

RIGHT
Britains set *119*, the Gloucestershire Regiment in Boer War foreign-service dress, firing, with early original box (**l, h**). *Phillips*

OPPOSITE BELOW
Britains set *31*, the 1st Dragoons, with a pleasingly designed box label. An attractive feature of early sets of dragoons and hussars is the throat plume that decorated the horse, a feature that was discontinued in 1909 and so is an indication of when a set was made. The set seen here sold for £700 in 1987, but this is above the normal price level for this set (**l, j**). *Phillips*

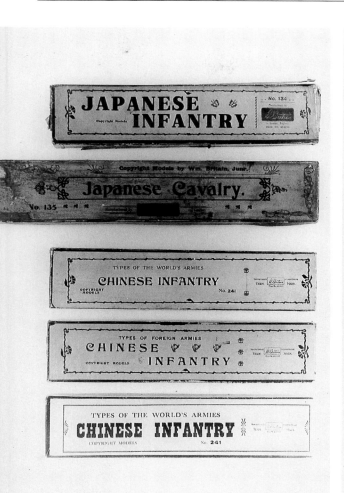

The discovery of a previously unknown toy soldier manufacturer is of great significance to collectors. This selection of figures complete with a number of the boxes, of which an example is shown, came in to Phillips for auction. Although the toys had previously been known to collectors, they had never been attributable to a particular manufacturer (**C**). *Phillips*

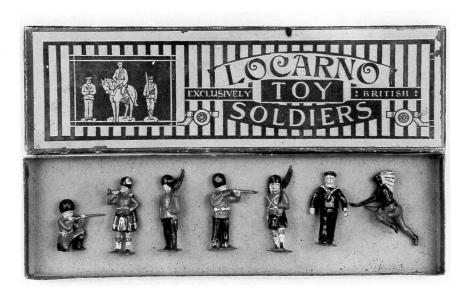

more difficult to find than the figures alone, and their rarity makes collecting them more of a challenge.

CONDITION AND DAMAGE

Undoubtedly the most attractive toy soldiers are those that are in as good condition as possible. There is a mystique about almost anything that is brand new and unused, partly because such an item has about it the anticipation of future use or enjoyment by its owner, and partly because it has also the sad inevitability of deterioration in the fullness of time. Conversely, the older that an object in mint condition becomes, the more remarkable and admirable that condition is seen to be. Britains toy soldiers in this condition dating from the 19th century command a premium far above their mid-20th-century successors, over and above the rarity of the figures themselves. As a rough guide, mint, boxed items from 1900 would be worth six times as much as a merely good set, while the equivalent difference for models produced in 1960 would be only just more than twice the price. From all periods, however, the rarer the models, the higher the premium on better condition.

While acting as consultant valuer to Phillips I have tried to evolve a system of describing soldiers that will provide common ground for collectors. First, the most recently arrived plastic sack filled with 1,200 broken figures by assorted manufacturers must be meticulously unwrapped. Then the basic objective is to sort out everything that is brought in to be sold into lots that will fetch a price of not less than about £30. Each lot has to be described in such a way that people who are not able to attend the auction can visualize what is in it, as well as pointing out features of interest to those who are viewing. Finally, the estimate is established as a guide to what might be a sensible bid.

The major problem connected with describing items is the definition of condition. What one collector might consider *good* (G), another collector might consider only *fair* (F). If you really cannot reach the auctions – and there is no substitute for viewing – then it is at least helpful if you understand what is going on in the valuer's mind when he is writing his descriptions. There is usually a great deal to be implied from the wording and data given. First, reproduced overleaf is the standard glossary to be found inside Phillips' auction catalogue.

One term on which everyone can agree is the definition of *mint* (M). This means an original set or item that has never been taken out of its box. The box also should be in pristine condition, the whole ensemble looking just as it would have done when it was purchased in the toyshop. Even here, a descriptive difficulty arises. When some mint boxes of Prairie Schooners arrived for auction, they had not even been taken out of the factory's outer wrappers, and the interior of the boxes could not be viewed without removing them. I believe a collector would have to be very strong willed not to take the factory wrapper off and look inside, so this was done before auction. Another problem arose because the corner of one of the boxes was torn. Strictly, this would mean the box was no longer mint, but it was so obviously factory-fresh that no lesser description would fit. The answer on such occasions is to describe that lot as "M. but box somewhat torn", which sounds contradictory but conveys the mint condition of the set while warning that the box is not intact. So now the term mint is used whenever the set has never been removed from its box, while any damage to the box or contents is described if necessary.

The description of each lot in the catalogue has to be kept as short as possible to save printing costs, which is why the system of abbreviations is so important. Ideally it would be better for the descriptions to be

GLOSSARY

Descriptions:

The following descriptions of paintwork are used in this catalogue:

M = Mint figures apparently never taken out of mint original boxes.

E = Excellent figures with no apparent paint chipping or defects.

G = Good figures with a minimum of scratches to the paint.

F = Fair figures with an acceptable amount of paint damage.

P = Poor figures probably suitable for repainting or restoration.

Where referring to boxes:

E = Excellent original box with no damage, complete with all interior fittings.

G = Good box with normal use wear only, but fittings not necessarily complete.

F = Fair box, possibly slightly torn or split, but with label intact.

P = Poor box, likely to be split or torn, and in need of repair.

Sets:

Where there is no reason to suppose that a particular group of figures is other than as sold together originally by the manufacturer it is described as a set. Buyers are warned that this opinion is necessarily a matter subject to speculation other than with MINT items. Sets that normally contain officers, trumpeters etc. are deemed to do so unless otherwise described.

Damage:

This is normally fully described in the text.

s.d. = slight damage, indicating that a small part such as a helmet spike, plume, bayonet, tail or hoof is missing. The general term "damage" is applied where more extensive damage is to be found. Manufacturers' original casting errors are not considered to be damage.

Repainting:

"Repainting" is where the figure has been altered markedly in colour from its original manufacturer's finish.

Where a figure is "repainted to" a certain uniform, the uniform quoted is that which now appears.

A figure that is "repainted from" a certain uniform, the uniform quoted is the original manufacturer's finish.

"Retouching" is an attempted restoration of the original manufacturer's finish.

"Minor retouching" means that less than 25% of this figure has been overpainted.

"Embellishment" is where additional features have been painted onto the original uniform and less than 25% of the figure has been overpainted.

"Minor Embellishment" indicates a minimum amount that does not detract from the original finish.

Lead Rot:

Where lead rot is described, this refers to a decomposition of the surface of the metal model sufficient to detract from its appearance. A leaflet on this phenomenon and storage conditions is available to clients.

Date:

The date given is our opinion as to when the item could have been manufactured, and is intended to provide a guide to the version that might be expected. Where no date is given the lot is mixed or the time of manufacture uncertain.

The Estimate:

The estimate is given in brackets near the end of each lot. The estimate gives the range of price that the lot is expected to reach.

Number of pieces:

The last figure in brackets at the end of the description is the number of pieces in the lot. All items are included, and where damage is specified all pieces are counted towards the total. Where riders are detachable a horse and rider count as one. Linked items such as gun teams count as the number of pieces of which they are composed, e.g. four horse wagon with two seated men count as seven (7). Vehicle drivers etc. count if removable from the vehicle. Where no number, or an approximate number, is given, the lot is offered as viewed.

Care is taken to ensure that any statement e.g. as to maker, set number, description and condition is reliable and accurate, but all such statements are statements of opinion.

(See also Buyers Conditions and Standard Conditions of Sale number 2.)

Britains *set 144a*, Royal Field Artillery in service dress. This is a second version, dating from about 1924, with light harness horses but still with two seated men on the limber. The set should also include a mounted officer, and it is also without its original box. Note that the side of the gun breach is missing (**H**). *Phillips*

longer. For instance, what is to be done when the paintwork of one figure out of a set is clearly in worse condition than the rest. It could be described "E but one F", or the whole set could be described as "G". Although the first description is technically correct, it could be taken to imply that the set does not match. The easiest lots to describe are the mint ones; the more damage there is, the more difficult it is to write the description.

As far as paintwork is concerned, "M" (mint) indicates no damage at all, although even here the packing cord or base card may have rubbed against the figures. "E" (excellent) also indicates no damage at all, but paint damage caused by trade distribution rather than by nursery play is allowable if unnoticeable. "E" items have that glossy, new look about them. "G" (good) applies to toys that have seen some service but have obviously been looked after. A few paint scratches or chips are acceptable, but the general first impression would be of a nice set. "F" (fair) items definitely look a bit worn but still have at least 75 per cent of their paint in position. Most collectors would agree that it would be a pity to repaint them. "P" (poor) items are anything that is worse than "F", down to no paint at all. "P" indicates that converting or repainting would be in order. A mixed description – e.g., G–F – indicates either that some of the figures in the lot are better than F or that the cataloguer could not make his mind up between the two. This effectively gives three extra categories – E–G, G–F and F–P – for these borderline cases.

When describing damage, an important distinction must be drawn between something broken and something missing. The word broken implies that the parts are still there and could be mended, as opposed to their being missing or gone. If a lot is simply described as damaged,

Britains *set 66*, the 1st Bombay Lancers, in its original early box. The box is obviously in bad shape, but early boxes are hard to come by (l, i). *Phillips*

Phillips recently sold an example of *set 131*, the largest set ever made by Britains, which originally contained 275 pieces. The price was £10,000 (in 1987), although this would have been considerably more had the box and contents been in better condition (**M**).

The special features of *set 131* were the items that were not sold by Britains in any other set: the Worcestershire Regiment running and marching (**l**); the British Camel Corps (**m**), of which there were nine in the box; and a Naval gun team with 12 men pulling a larger limber, the men being soldered to the draw wires (**l**). One man is missing from this team.

When figures like these are for sale apart from in the set as a whole, they fetch far more proportionately than the rest. For instance, a single British Camel Corps figure fetched £250 in 1981, and eight figures from the Worcestershire Regiment fetched £800 in 1987. *Phillips*

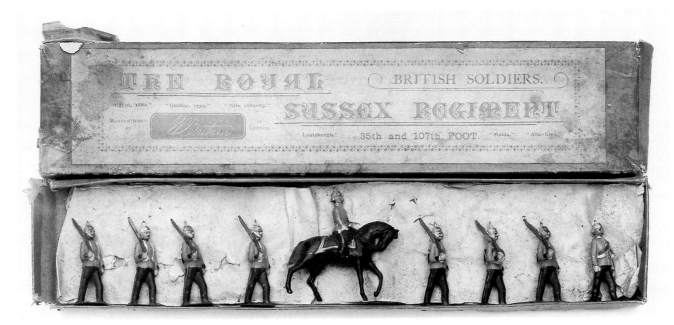

Britains set *36*, the Royal Sussex Regiment, is here shown with both a mounted and a foot officer. The box is in rather poor condition, but, as no set number is included in the design of the label, it must date before 1898. The contents came with a large quantity of other Sussex Regiment figures, and it will never be totally certain if these are the correct contents for this box. Normally, Britains would include only one officer, the mounted one, in this box, but it has been known to have been issued with just the foot officer. It is also possible that the foot officer belonged to *set 19*, the West India Regiment. This box was sold for £500 in 1984 (J). *Phillips*

distressed or "a.f." (as found), the damage is, in the cataloguer's opinion, too complicated to be described in detail given the value of the item concerned. Postal bidders on these items should bear in mind that the damage could be very extensive, so bids are a gamble. The cataloguer is, in effect, saying that you must look at this yourself before bidding.

The number of items in the lot is also important. If a lot of soldiers is counted, it makes it easier to infer whether it constitutes a set or not. Equally, it gives better protection against one of the pieces being stolen, for no one could tell if the lot had not previously been counted. Where a lot is simply designated as "a lot", it usually means that the pieces in it are numerous, of low value and/or open to question as to quantity. It might, for instance, be difficult to count 5,000 Airfix 20mm scale war-gaming troops. If there are several different connected parts to something, as in a stage coach and team, or detachable riders or accessories, with some loose, the count becomes complicated. It has in the past been the practice to discount badly damaged pieces altogether, but this could give a totally false impression of a lot, so now it seems better to count all of them and state damage, rather than ignore them.

The date given for a lot is a further indication of what to expect by way of a version of a figure, rather than a totally accurate date of its manufacture. The date is set clearly within one of the time periods set out on page 51, so that it is evident whether the figures have, for instance, gaiters or full trousers. A version or type of figure that is particularly interesting will usually be referred to in the description, and when an item seems unusual, the cataloguer will probably draw attention to it by calling it *rare*.

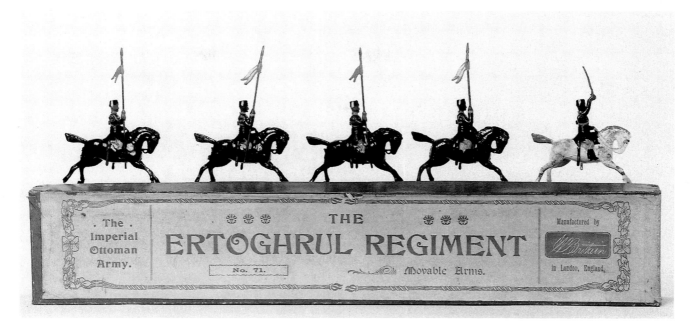

Britains *set 71*, the Turkish Cavalry – during the early years the box label named the regiment of the Turkish Army that was represented, and it is rare to find the set with this box (**H, j**). *Phillips*

The definitions from "E" (excellent) through "G" (good) and "F" (fair) to "P" (poor) are applied separately to the figures and box, where there is one. Any description other than *mint* implies that the figures have been taken out of the box, even if they are now restrung. In such instances there is always the risk that the figures are not in the original box in which they were first sold, which is not always an easy fault to detect. Any collector who likes the intricate printing of the box labels will want to collect the boxes to go with his figures, or, if he has empty boxes, he will want to fill them. Putting matching sets and boxes together is a difficult collecting skill, and problems often arise when a deceased collector's property is described.

The normal test of a complete set is simply to check that the paintwork matches from figure to figure throughout the set, within the limits used by the manufacturer. For instance, Britains Danish Hussar officer coat was sometimes a lighter red than the troopers' (I have seen two mint boxed sets like this). Equally, it is well established that the base of the 1905 dated infantry officer was changed from an oval to a square earlier than the base of the box-pack infantryman, so that there are genuine sets of oval-based men with a square-based officer. The set must also match the box in period, the parts of the box must demonstrably fit together, and the card insert to which the figures were once strung, if present, must have the correct number of holes for the number of figures in the set. Here one has to allow for the possibility that the top and bottom of the box may have led separate existences for a time; for example, if the set in its box was displayed in a window without the lid, the bottom of the box (the tray) might have been faded by the sun, but the top of the box would still be dark. Figures within a set may also have suffered from faded paint, and, if one figure is turned over, it may look completely different from the rest of the set.

Where there is reasonable doubt over the matching of the set, the lot description reads "from set 32" rather than "set 32". Where the box does not appear to match the set, the description will read "in an original box" rather than "in original box"

The definition of a set is a group of figures and/or accessories that was originally offered for sale by the manufacturer in a single package. Once figures have been taken out of their box there is no guarantee that they are really a set. It is reasonable to assume, however, if there are no grounds for suspicion, that when there is a box with a correct number of figures, they were originally a set.

Further difficulties arise when there are more figures than needed. If there are enough to make two sets, how can they be sorted correctly if they are the same style and version? If different paint styles are obvious, the description will state "two figures do not match", but even after allowing for some of the regular peculiarities like those mentioned above, some seeming non-matches can be correct. After all, Britains employed many painters, and there were inevitably differences in style between them – the thickness of moustaches and crossbelts, for example. The marvel is that the style was so consistent. However, it was normal practice for the same painter to complete all the figures in a set, even when they included different castings.

Also be on the look out for mixed versions; some cavalry sets – the Middlesex Yeomanry, for instance – had one or two different troopers in the set at some periods. When examining the paintwork, look for different shades of base colour, the placement of helmet insignia and the style of face painting (all should be with or without eyebrows, for example). If the style of paint is totally consistent, this enhances the chances of a group of figures being a genuine set.

The vast majority of sets sold at auction are genuine, for they have only passed through the hands of the original purchaser from the shop where they were bought. A collector may well have tried to improve the quality of a boxed set – e.g., by replacing a broken figure with an unbroken one – and then, when selling, may have forgotten that he did so. Alternatively, of course, sorting out vast quantities of figures, the cataloguer himself may get it wrong.

REPAIR AND RESTORATION

There are several purposes behind repairing and repainting toy soldiers, all very much a matter of personal taste for the collector. First, there is the decision whether to do any work at all, since there is certainly a value attached to toy figures in original condition. My own view is that I would never touch a figure of which I had not already got a better example, otherwise I would lose my only record of what the original colours were, and that my decision would otherwise depend on the appearance of the figure – is it in fit condition to join the ranks on display or in such a poor state that only refurbishment will allow it to take part?

Once you have decided which figures to work on, you will probably adopt one of two main approaches: restoring as nearly as possible to the original paint or repainting in the general style of Britains.

Restoring a figure as nearly as possible to its original paint is the most difficult and painstaking work, particularly if there is no original to work to. Most restorers start by stripping the entire figure to the bare metal and then applying artists' enamels, carefully mixed to the exact shades. I know of only a dozen people capable of exactly reproducing Britains original paint, and with these, detection is possible only under ultraviolet light. Since the hours of work involved are usually far beyond the cost of obtaining good, original figures, such work is undertaken usually for the challenge of producing an exact replica.

If achieving restoration standard is not necessary, stripping off and repainting figures can be both relatively quick and a most satisfying way of building up a smart army at low cost. A great deal of fun may be had by exchanging heads and arms to achieve models that Britains never made originally, thereby occasionally causing the hearts of serious collectors to miss a beat when they momentarily think they are seeing a Britains figure of which they were previously unaware. Many of this type of model can be used to enhance cameo or campaign collections (see Chapters 8 and 9). Arms can be changed by gently forcing the movable arms off their existing pegs and pressing them back onto different ones. When arms are missing, new ones may be had at a modest price from companies that cast spare arms and advertise in the toy soldier magazines. New heads are also obtainable and are an easy way of completely altering a figure's appearance. Many toy soldier manufacturers used the idea of inter-changeable heads to make various regiments, and indeed most German and French solid-cast figures have heads, made with a plug to fit into the neck, that may readily be taken off.

Nicely repainted figures have a considerably higher value than originals in poor condition, unless, that is, the originals are exceptionally rare. Well-executed military bands, for instance, made up of Britains figures repainted to a standard a little better than the average Britains figure, can fetch (in 1987) £5 to £8 per figure at auction.

Retouching figures, that is, the filling in of scratches or chips with an attempted match of colour, is almost invariably unsuccessful and reduces the value. Before the current rise in prices some adult collectors used to embellish their figures with insignia of rank, such as chevrons, or extra uniform detail, such as shoulder straps. If very neatly done and not too evident, these embellishments do not seem to affect the value too much, but ultimately such figures must be considered as blemished.

Finally there is the question of repair. Any repair work that needs to be carried out on a poor figure cannot but be advantageous. With good condition, original sets, however, the decision to repair is more difficult. Sets in which one figure is missing an arm or one horse a tail or leg do not

A Turkish detachment in the style of Britains The cavalry and the rear rank of infantry on guard are the original Britains, but the charging and lying infantry are by Alex Riches, who sometimes makes superb extrapolations of what Britains might have done. Here he has added a bayonet and Turkish head to the Britains Serbian figure. The rest of the figures are by conversion from other Britains figures of repainted Turks (**e**). The gun is by Mark Time. *Author's collection*

look nearly as good as those sets that are complete. The difference in price is considerable, as well. My own view is that the minimum repair necessary to make a figure stand up is all that should be done. Others often feel that it is well worth while to do a proper job of repair and painting in over the top. Such work, if well done, can be missed on resale, but if it is badly done, can affect the price adversely. A prospective purchaser should always examine figures carefully to see if there are any hairline cracks at the neck or slight bulges in horses' legs that might denote glued or soldered repairs rather than an unbroken original.

Occasionally sets of re-cast figures are offered for sale, sometimes so meticulously painted in the Britains style that they deceive the closest inspection. If you pick up a re-cast figure you will instantly detect if it is heavier than the normal hollow-cast equivalent, since re-casting is nearly always done as a solid cast.

ACQUIRING IMPERFECT FIGURES

Lead rot, *poor* condition or damage all make figures cheaper to buy, and it must be a personal choice whether to buy only the finest examples or whether to sacrifice quality for quantity. Toy soldiers are one of the few collectable objects where it is quite justifiable to choose the latter, since the more toy soldiers are on parade, the better they look. For those with a practical bent, the restoration or repainting of damaged soldiers is an absorbing pastime and, as long as the soldiers did not cost much at auction to start with, usually adds to the value (see page 128). It is not usually possible, however, to recover the full cost of the time spent on "doing up" figures well, nor is it possible to predict with any certainty the price that will be obtained.

The other major reason for buying an imperfect figure is as a substitute until a perfect example can be found; however, some figures are so rare that only imperfect examples are known to exist.

6
COLLECTING DECISIONS

My own approach to collecting has changed at various times throughout my life as I have made a series of decisions about the direction that my collection should take. Nothing stays the same, and a decision that appeared to be right at one time may well, in different circumstances, require an alternative response.

Decisions are to do with the ultimate objective, that is, the completion of the collection, and that includes the way in which it is presented to the world as a statement of the collector and the story that it has to tell. Often, as a collection grows, a part of it will suddenly stand out as not belonging to the whole any more, and this can then either form a subsidiary collection or be sold to finance the continuing growth of the central entity.

This development is apparent in many of the major collections round the world. I have been privileged to help with the formation of some of the foremost, including, for instance, that of my friend Ed Ruby in Orange County, California. Ed started collecting with the residue of a stock of Britains that he was selling retail in his ironmongery store in Chicago, and his taste has varied into Mignot, connoisseur models and Nostalgia series. As the core of his collection, Britains figures, in all their intriguing versions and mellow early paintings, has grown, he has gradually divested himself of all distractions except a few personal favourites and concentrated on showing the diversity and interest of the Britains within a single, fully glass-shelved room. He has not all that many more Britains acquisitions to make – a few of the 1940 buildings, parade sets, Paris Office figures, specials and a few still missing versions. Part of the fun in knowing Ed is in the challenge to think of aspects of Britains that he has not yet thought of collecting, or even that he has not suspected exist. In spite of all the items that I could conjecture might exist and that Ed does not yet have, his collection of Britains remains the finest I have ever seen or heard about.

My own first collecting decision was to attempt to acquire the entire output of the British and Hong Kong toy soldier manufacturers in plastic. I set this objective in 1962, and I scoured the toyshops and toy fairs to try to keep up with everything that was being produced. The plethora of figures produced in plastic was, even then, past its peak, and only Britains, Timpo, Cherilea, Charbens and Lone Star were making the running against a flood of cheap copies from Hong Kong. Even here, limiting decisions had to be made: for instance, I excluded all civilian items and cowboys (although not Indians), and when series of figures were sold loose in counter packs as well as in boxed sets, I tended just to get one of each figure.

This state of affairs continued until 1973, by which time all but Timpo, Cherilea and Britains had dropped out of the market, and manufacturers tended to produce big playsets with added accessories. If I had kept to my stated purpose, I would have been forced to buy large quantities of duplicates in order to get the accessories included in the larger boxes, for which much of the money went into the packaging itself anyway. The variety of packaging was becoming alarming, while the range of figures was becoming less imaginative. I found myself becoming bored.

Symptoms of boredom in collecting are usually manifested in a reluctance to go on purchasing according to a particular plan, and this should prompt a long hard think about directions. During the same period, 1962–73, I had also been interested in war-gaming, in painting my own figures and in becoming familiar with all the old metal figures, which I had been purchasing from time to time. I found I wanted to try to collect as many as possible of the figures, made in whatever material, that had been produced in Britain between 1893 and 1973. This gave full rein to my emerging interest in early Britains, and saved my spending any more on repetitive sets of plastic figures.

From then on I went to the auctions to build up my Britains collection and fill in many of the other makes such as Reka, B.M.C., Hill and Crescent. I started to acquire all the different boxed sets by Britains that I could, and I was a real collector by set number, trying to get one of each number, then one of each version and often variations as well. I divided Britains output into 30 subject areas and tried to fill them all.

The 30 subject areas are:

(1) royalty;
(2) Household Cavalry;
(3) Foot Guards;
(4) Dragoon Guards and dragoons;
(5) hussars;
(6) lancers;
(7) Infantry of the Line;
(8) Highlanders;
(9) other British infantry in full dress;
(10) Royal Artillery;
(11) Royal Navy and Marines;
(12) auxiliary services and Royal Air Force;
(13) Boer War;
(14) troops in khaki (from both world wars);
(15) vehicles (motor) and guns;
(16) Indian Empire;
(17) Canada;
(18) rest of the British Empire;
(19) France;
(20) rest of Europe;
(21) Asia and Africa;
(22) United States of America;
(23) Latin America;
(24) historical;
(25) American Civil War, cowboys and Indians;
(26) buildings;
(27) civilians;
(28) Picture Packs;
(29) small size and
(30) second grade.

Britains *set 1869*, the Royal Army Medical Corps casualty clearing station, with thatched barn and open cart shed. This was one of a series of superb model buildings made for Britains by Hugar, a small firm of craftsmen model makers. An interesting addition to Britains' range of buildings is the additional items in a similar style put out under the Hugar trademark. The cardboard used for the roof of this particular building is made from the underside of printed board for the box of the Snow White cottage, and a dwarf can just be seen illustrated on the lower edge of the eve to the right (J). *Phillips*

Each of these subject areas is large enough to make an interesting mini-collection in its own right, and within each are rare items that need plenty of searching out. Picture packs, small size and second-grade figures contain items from a number of areas, but I believe they form better collecting subjects on their own.

During the period 1973–80, my collection reached its peak, and I felt satisfied that most of my plan had been accomplished. Since I was no longer in the market in a major way, I was able to take up the opportunity to become consultant cataloguer for toy soldiers at Phillips Auctioneers, London, and this swung my interests yet further towards the compilation and dissemination of information about toy soldiers, and to thoughts of how my own collection, now that it had been amassed, should evolve.

Deciding what has to go is probably the most painful part of any collector's life, but it can also be a very positive process. First, I divided up everything, apart from the Britains figures, into similar subject areas.

DISPLAYS (See Chapter 8)

(31) Fusiliers;
(32) Scots Greys;
(33) Boer War;
(34) Boxer Rebellion;
(35) Sudan;
(36) boyhood army;
(37) field manoeuvres;
(38) castles;
(39) coronation procession;
(40) Indian Army.

METAL BRITISH TOY SOLDIERS
OTHER THAN BRITAINS HOLLOW-CAST

(41) pre-World War I;
(42) Hill;
(43) between the world wars;
(44) Timpo;
(45) Crescent;
(46) post-World War II
(47) unknowns;
(48) Wend-Al and Aluminium;
(49) die-casts
(50) artillery.

A miscellany of figures. Top row: the second from left is a Comet Zouave (**c**) made in the United States; the group of five charging figures (**e**) of various nations of World War I is interesting but of unknown make; at the far right is a Japanese-made Minikin figure of a Lowlander (**e**).

Middle row: the first figure is a model from a collectors' set issued by a mail order house – these are almost invariably overpriced and have little resale value (**c**); next is a figure of King John, made for Graham Farrish by Russell Gammage (**f**) and this is followed by a Courtenay model of Queen Elizabeth I (**h**), with a damaged sceptre. The next figure is a Ping model of Oliver Cromwell (**e**), followed by three Carman figures (**d**) and a group of French hollow-cast casualties with shellburst, medical staff and radio operator (**e**); finally, a French hollow-cast figure depicting a British colour bearer of World War I (**e**).

On the bottom row is a variety of figures, the third and fourth from the left being by Mignot (**e**); the sixth was made of plaster in Britain (**b**), and the seventh and eighth, a swagman and a duck-billed platypus (**c**) come from Australia, and the last figure is a flamboyant French hollow-cast figure (**f**).

Author's collection

PLASTIC BRITISH TOY SOLDIERS

(51) Britains and Herald;
(52) Timpo;
(53) Charbens;
(54) Cherilea;
(55) Airfix;
(56) Marx;
(57) Hong Kong;
(58) Lone Star;
(59) Others;
(60) Vehicles and guns.

OTHER COLLECTIONS

(61) Blenheim/Nostalgia;
(62) New Toy Soldiers;
(63) soldiers of the world;
(64) fire engines;
(65) toys;
(66) Lego;
(67) souvenirs;
(68) war-gaming.

This exercise provided a framework within which to work and an opportunity to rationalize everything that I had amassed into the essential, the nostalgic, the bulky and the unattractive. The sorted list then needed further consideration: Which items was I least fond of? Which items did people know about already, so that I did not need to keep them to demonstrate with? Which items would be worth selling?

The solution that I arrived at is the same that any collector must reach unless he has the money and space to collect the entire range of, for instance, Britains – specialization. If one had the whole Britains range, any specialist collection that one wanted to demonstrate within the range could be brought out. Short of that, I had to decide what range of specialist collections would satisfy my collecting instincts while leaving me free to live in comfort. Between 1980 and 1986, these decisions were taken. Of the 30 subjects of Britains, I reduced the majority to a skeleton collection, the barest minimum of figures that would still enable me to demonstrate something of what that subject was about. One can demonstrate the entire range of Britains Indian Army (for instance), with just four figures – the cavalryman, the Bikanir Camel Corps, the infantryman at the trail with pack and the infantryman at the slope without pack. All the sets and specials that one could collect are variations and paintings of these.

I wanted to keep some subjects intact in order to demonstrate what a full collection could be if similar depth were extended across all subjects. The intact subjects I still have are: 1, 8, 17, 23, 24, 25, 28, 29 and 30. Subject 1, royalty, effectively forms part of display subject 39, coronation procession, so I did not want to lose it. Subject 8, Highlanders, a favourite with many collectors, is now the only British Army subject area that I am continuing to try to complete. Areas 17, 23 and 24 are relatively small collections of Britains, which I had more or less completed and which seemed well worth keeping. Areas 28, the Picture Packs, and 29, the small size figures, had long been particular favourites of mine, and 25 and 30, relatively neglected areas of Britains collecting, were, for that reason, not worth getting rid of, for not only would I lose collections of potential curiosity value but also the lack of interest in them would mean the value realized would be very low.

As far as the rest of the collection was concerned, I decided that the display collections would have to be severely curtailed. I realized that I had already collected enough pieces to keep me busy converting and repainting beyond my hundred and twentieth birthday and so had better release some of them for other people to complete. Thus, subjects 33, 35, 37 and 40 were cut back to already finished items, and an impending further subject, the Zulu War, was also disposed of.

For the rest of the subjects, my new ruling is that instead of striving for completion and acquiring anything and everything that I have not already collected, I limit myself to the best representation of the range for the purposes of my three principles of collecting: demonstration, nostalgia and agreeability. Many of the subjects under consideration have not yet been culled, but worthwhile portions of subjects 49, 51, 52, 56, 61, 63 and 64 have already left the fold, leaving the rest in a more available, memorable and attractive state.

The story continues, for my collection will continue to evolve or it would not otherwise continue to hold my interest. Of all that there is to collect within the definition of toy soldiers, my original "British" idea probably limited me to about one tenth, and my current limit is about a quarter of that. Even while I am refining my earlier acquisitions, I am still collecting from time to time items that enhance the subjects I still have or that add highlights to the ones I have reduced.

Large-scale figures.

The seventh figure from the left in the centre row is 54mm scale. This illustration shows the incredible variety that can be collected within any theme that can be devised. Top row, left to right: five aluminium Norse warriors by Krolyn (**f**); three Argyll and Sutherland Highlanders made of composition by Elastolin (**h**); three Papal State Swiss Guards and one Noble Guard made of plaster composition in Italy (**d**); five dime-store figures (**f**), of which the first is a green plastic copy of a dime-store figure, made in Brazil, and the second is a modern reproduction of a dime-store figure; finally, a mounted Norman, riding down a Saxon as at the battle of Hastings (**e**) – in my opinion, Elastolin produced even better figures in plastic (as here) than it had done in composition.

Centre row, left to right: a lithographed flat tin figure with stand-up tabs (**e**); a hollow die-cast infantryman (**b**); an Italian ski trooper made of aluminium (**f**); a composition figure made by Leyla in Germany (**d**); a reproduction of an Elastolin personality figure of General Ludendorff (**c**); an unpainted plastic Roman carrying the axe and fasces made by Atlantic (**a**); a fixed-arm Zang Products British Foot Guard (**c**), which, with modifications, went into the Herald range; a hollow soldier made of two sides of pressed tinplate joined together with tabs (**e**); a large scale Heyde British Foot Guard (**h**); a tall, semi-flat Greek Evzone (**b**); wooden French standard bearers of the Imperial Guard and 1916 infantry (**h**); a wooden figure of Garibaldi from Italy (**g**) a

Mattel G.I. hero in plastic (**a**), which is an early example of the large scale plastic action figures such as Masters of the Universe that now dominate the toyshops – this one has a lever that causes the waist to swivel with a clicking sound simulating the emission of a swath of bullets; and finally an Italian-made Alpini ski trooper (**d**), which is made of foam rubber.

Bottom row, from left to right: two composition Belgian Grenadiers *à cheval*, made in Belgium by Durso (**h**); eight composition figures (**d**) made in Denmark, although the horses are metal, to depict the Danish Livgard, with the figure on the right of the group being King Christiansen (**f**); finally, a large hollow-cast toy soldier of unknown provenance (**f**). *Author's collection*

7
SPECIALIZATION

Having looked at a case study – my own collection – it is time to review a selection of the almost infinite variety of forms that collections take. Among the multitude of collecting themes are: (1) by manufacturer; (2) by country of origin; (3) universal collections – i.e., acquiring whatever can be obtained or "magpie" collecting; (4) by type of production – i.e., solid, hollow-cast, flat, etc.; (5) by scale; (6) by period of manufacture – e.g., before 1900; (7) by subject, regimental, historical event, etc.; (8) by personal association – e.g., regiment in which one served; (9) by nostalgia – i.e., those toy soldiers in the shops when one was young; (10) by catalogue number or any sub-division thereof; or (11) by point of interest: the cameo collection.

COLLECTING BY MANUFACTURER
Chapter 2 gave a brief résumé of the processes by which toy soldiers have been made and which manufacturers used which processes. When collectors compare their collections, their first point of contact is usually "which manufacturers do you collect?" The response might be that one had various Britains, a few Mignot, a nice assortment of Barclay and a quantity of Lineol. This instantly establishes common ground.

Collecting by manufacturer is probably the most common form of collecting, if only because the various products of one manufacturer usually fit better with each other than mixed with the products of other makers. It is true that even those new products that attempt to complement old figures nevertheless have a style all their own that looks better massed apart than mingled with older figures. Different manufacturers tend not to be compatible. Even within the range of a single manufacturer, there are incongruities, and when a firm has been producing for as long as Britains, there are bound to be several distinguishable styles and groups that do not really stand well with each other. By and large, the better manufacturers produced more consistent products than the more down-market operators; the figures of Crescent, for instance, often fit no better with each other than with those of its competitors.

Modern firms producing for the collector have not improved on their old counterparts, although they tend to strive for some constancy of scale or design. Sometimes there is an active desire to be different; for instance, Blenheim decided to make all its figures march with the other foot forward than is shown in Britains usual pose.

This selection of Britains specials of full-dress types of the British Army in peak caps (j) was produced as part of a mechanical coronation procession commissioned by the City of Edinburgh in 1953. *Phillips*

George V – an individual boxed figure from Heyde about 1912 (j). *Phillips*

This set contains figures supplied by Britains to another distributor, which boxed them up and sold the set under its own name. The Army Service Supply Column is a rare and attractive set dating from about 1906. A similar set to this was sold at Phillips, New York, in 1986 for $11,000 (**M**). *Phillips*

One fascinating exposition of toy soldiers is to contrast all the various styles by collecting examples from as many manufacturers as possible. Here it is instructive to compare their various attempts at depicting one type of uniform, such as a Foot Guard or a Highlander. It is evident that master figures were made for the less consistent manufacturers by a number of designers, and sometimes the work of different manufacturers goes together better than other products by the same firm. One might detect the hand of one designer working for two employers here, and examples of this are known. Cherington created designs for Hill, Charbens, Crescent and Cherilea, and Selwyn Smith made models for Timpo and Herald. When firms pirated the Timpo and Herald combat infantry designs and produced copies of both ranges together, the blend was almost indistinguishable because the same person had originated both ranges.

Most collectors embrace a range of manufacturers, but the output of each of the following runs into over a thousand separate models and so would be large enough to form sizeable collections in itself: Britains, Mignot, Lucotte, Heyde, Heinrichsen, Elastolin, Lineol, Marx and Timpo. In contrast, it would also be possible to form a considerable conversation-piece collection of figures not yet identified to *any* manufacturer!

COLLECTING BY COUNTRY OF ORIGIN

There is a marked propensity for collectors in a country to collect the toy soldiers that were distributed in that country when they were young. This

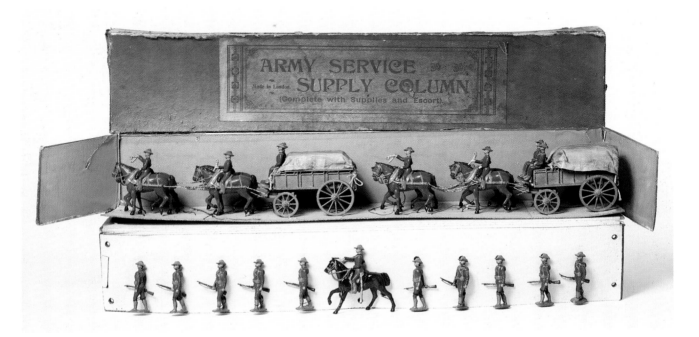

is one area where the saying "a prophet is without honour in his own country" is not applicable. Almost invariably, the largest group of collectors for any toy soldier manufacturer is found in the country in which that manufacturer was mostly originally sold, and many collectors like to group these manufacturers together by country of origin. The three major originating countries are Germany, France and Britain, but Italy, Spain and more recently Hong Kong would also afford scope for fascinating collections. John G. Garratt's *The World Encyclopedia of Model Soldiers* is very useful for forming such collections, and it lists, for instance, 22 countries where commercial plastic figures have been made, 18 where solids were made and 9 where hollow-cast were produced. Additional information, however, turns up all the time as collectors write to magazines about their own discoveries.

THE UNIVERSAL COLLECTION

The most satisfying way to start collecting toy soldiers is to buy those items that seem to be particularly attractive. Most collectors go through an acquisitive, "magpie" stage, during which they sample all sorts of items and taste the flavour of different makes and types.

Perhaps the most famous magpie collector was the late John Hanington, whose collection, although containing highlights such as his superb Lucottes and his theme of military medical services, could not be said to have excluded any area of toy soldier manufacture whatsoever. He was interested in and appreciated all of them, and he was prepared to buy what appealed to him. The result was a most intriguing mixture of items

A similar figure of George V in a larger scale than the figure seen opposite, possibly also by Heyde (1). The saddle and cloth, which was cast as a separate piece, is missing. *Phillips*

Britains set *2017*, an interesting novelty item, the ski troops were first produced shortly after World War II. The slung rifles are a separate casting and can be found painted white. These figures have recently become very popular among collectors and cost up to £100 each (1). *Phillips*

on a grand scale, which was always a great treat to view on the several occasions on which his house in Wimbledon was thrown open to members of the British Model Soldier Society. Writing the catalogue of his collection for the executors' sale in May 1984 was a highly educational experience for me, and it was the first time that I had been able to examine large numbers of Lucottes, German solids and composition figures.

Collections that start out in this universal way tend to become specialized by sheer pressure of space, unless, of course, the resources of Malcolm Forbes are behind it. The Forbes collection, probably the world's finest, is also a universal one, but it aims to be thoroughly representative in all areas. Containing as it does over 70,000 figures, it would seem likely to have achieved this ambition, but there are also many fine models on display at the collection's home in the Palais Mendoub in Tangier. Peter and Anne Johnson, who are the museum curators, spend many hours tracking down unusual items. Nor can it be said that the effort of the craftsman is ignored, for the collection includes the battalion of the London Scottish that was put together on a man-for-man basis in the toy soldier style by an enthusiast interested in the battalion's exploits in World War I – each man in the battalion was identified and named.

There are ways of organizing a universal collection so that it is limited in size without losing its universal nature. For instance, it is possible to adopt the simple discipline of never having more than a certain number of figures, of never duplicating a figure, or of limiting the representation of any size, type or country to, say, the proportion of population, size of army and so forth. This is where the collector's ingenuity has to show itself. All these limitations can be the basis of fascinating stories about the collection when it is displayed.

COLLECTING BY TYPE OF PRODUCTION

A collection that is based on the type of production is another way of grouping manufacturers together, and, since the origin and continuance of types of production are usually with one country and the allegiance of collectors is also with one country, the type of production collection lends itself also to being a sub-division of a country's production. The distinct types of production are described in Chapter 2. The collection that endeavours to show examples of all the possible ways of producing toy soldiers is very interesting to assemble.

COLLECTING BY SCALE

All miniaturizations from real life are done to a particular scale. This can be expressed as a fraction of real life – e.g. 1/32, which means that a man six foot tall is depicted at 72/32 inches = 2⅛in; or 1/72, which means that the same man is depicted at exactly 1in tall.

The standard way in which toy soldier scale is reckoned is by the height of a hatless man in millimetres. The 2⅛in tall man then becomes 54mm, which is the way that Britains standard scale is usually expressed. Headgear or being mounted can make a big difference to the height of a figure, so conformity to a scale is important when describing a figure without being able to show it. The thickness of bases is also left out of the scale reckoning, and with composition figures this can add as much as 5mm ($\frac{1}{5}$in) to the height.

Given that in real life, men's heights will differ even in the best ordered armies, it is quite possible to collect soldiers within a range of 60mm down to 50mm scale and find that they look reasonably compatible. This is, after all, only the difference between men 6ft and 5ft tall. The different style of designs of the toys is likely to be far more noticeable than the differences in height when they are on display.

One way to form a collection within relatively narrow bounds, therefore, is to collect in one of the less widely used scale ranges; for instance, 40mm to 48mm would include the small Elastolins and Lineols, the prolific, but hard to acquire, output in this scale from Heyde and other German solid-cast manufacturers, and the smaller size B and W series from Britains.

COLLECTING BY PERIOD OF MANUFACTURE
Another limiting factor in the formation of a collection is the setting of dates of origin. The dates I set for myself were 1893 to 1973, which covered the first 80 years of British hollow-cast production. A limit of pre-1900 production would be very difficult to collect. Britains production and that of some other manufacturers such as Elastolin fall naturally into eras (see pages 45–51), and the era that most collectors turn to most readily is that of their youth.

COLLECTING BY SUBJECT
A vast number of historical subjects lend themselves to forming the subject of a collection. Most popular are the various different sorts of armed services – cavalry, artillery, medical services, Highlanders, military music or vehicles, for example. Individual regiments with their uniforms through their history would be difficult to collect in toy soldiers and are a better subject for a modeller. Medieval or ancient warriors, or cowboys and Indians, on the other hand, would be good toy soldier subjects. Individual wars, campaigns, battles or parades are all possible, and some of these subjects are discussed elsewhere in the book (see page 97, Boer War and other campaigns; pages 100–1, Royal Welch Fusiliers).

Subject collections can be vast even though limited to a single subject, since the acquisition of large numbers of similar figures is often the right way to give a good impression. On the other hand, subjects may be narrow enough to form collections of personal association or cameos (see pages 95–105).

COLLECTING BY PERSONAL ASSOCIATION
It often happens that there are associations, either personal or within the immediate family or ancestry, with certain arms of the military. Many

Britains set *129* contained 14 figures each of an example of the five different types of cavalry in the British Army. Left to right: the 2nd Life Guards, the 1st King's Dragoon Guards, the Royal Scots Greys 2nd Dragoons, the 11th Hussars and the 12th Lancers. *Author's collection*

collectors who have served in the army naturally feel the urge to collect their regiment in miniature. At one further remove, it is interesting to collect any unit with recruiting or name associations with the area in which the collector lives or grew up. Each of these personal associations is another point of interest to add to a collection, which can be enhanced, perhaps, by groups of inherited campaign medals or by old family photographs.

COLLECTING FOR NOSTALGIA

Nostalgia for the soldiers one had as a child is one of the most powerful collecting motives of all, and it is the closest personal association that one can have with toy soldiers, since that is probably the time of life when there was the most opportunity to enjoy them. I count myself extremely lucky in having retained most of the troops I had as a boy, although I wish I had not been quite such an enthusiastic embellisher of them. Even now, however, I have the urge to enhance regiments that I had then by filling them out to the numbers that I could not then afford. Luckily, my boyhood armies were mostly composed of the cheaper Crescent and Hill figures, which are still relatively inexpensive to collect today.

COLLECTING BY CATALOGUE

Catalogues are the manufacturers' listings of their products, and they are the most important source material from which to discover what was made by whom. Collecting by catalogue is the pursuit of all the numbers in a catalogue of soldiers or a section thereof, and the assumption is that what was listed in a catalogue is what was available on a regular basis at the time that catalogue was issued.

To collect all the catalogue numbered sets from a manufacturer is an interesting method of setting a goal and also the easiest method of knowing when a collection is complete. Britains Ltd issued extensive catalogues and meticulously numbered almost its whole production, which is one reason why its figures are so extensively collected. It is relatively easy to discover, for example, when any subject area within the Britains range is complete, at least in the sense that one of every catalogue number depicting that subject has been acquired.

Manufacturers' original catalogues can form a collection in themselves, and they are much sought after. I have always been fascinated by catalogues, by the thoughts of the manufacturer that they reveal, by the inconsistencies and inaccuracies that sometimes occur in them and by the pattern of production that they reveal when put in sequence.

To my knowledge, Britains catalogues or lists exist for the years 1902, 1904, 1909, 1915 and 1926, for every year from 1931 to 1941 and from 1946 to the present day. It is probable that a list or catalogue was issued for every year, or at even more frequent intervals, from 1893 onwards. The years I have not mentioned were either war years with no toy production or years for which the listings have not yet come to light.

I have written at length on Britains catalogue numbering in my book

Britains *set 29* in this four-row display box (**L**) comprises: (top right) the 1st Life Guards (**h**); (top and bottom left) the 3rd Hussars; (second row) the Mountain Artillery (**G**); (third row) the Royal West Surrey Regiment (**g**); and (bottom right) the 9th Lancers (**i**). *Phillips*

The large box contains Britains *set 129*, 14 figures each of five regiments of cavalry: (top left) the Royal Scots Greys 2nd Dragoons; (centre above and below) the 2nd Life Guards; (top right) the 11th Hussars; (below left) the 12th Lancers; and (below right) the 1st King's Dragoon Guards (**M, i**). *Phillips*

Britains Toy Soldiers 1893–1932 (see Bibliography). For quick reference, remember that the best quality standard scale military set numbers run from *1* to *500*, *1201* to *1918* and *2001* to *2189*; for a summary of the chronological issue of the sets, see page 49. Once a set had been given a number, it retained that number until it was dropped from the catalogue; therefore, the 1st Life Guards were *set 1* from 1893 until 1962, when a new numbering system, in which the metal military sets were in the range *9000* to *9999*, was introduced. It is fascinating to observe that although *set 1* remained *set 1* for 70 years, the figures making up *set 1* were often improved, and the packaging, paint style and labelling changed, so that a whole series of *sets 1* can be collected, each one in the series being slightly different from the one before. I call this a sequence of sets.

All the major manufacturers issued catalogues. I have found original or reprinted catalogues for Elastolin, Lineol, Hill (Johillco), Crescent, Wend-Al, Lone Star, Taylor & Barratt, Cherilea, Timpo, Marx, Mignot, Heyde, Lucottes, Authenticast, Swedish African Engineers, Charbens and Segal. Reprinted catalogues are stocked by dealers and advertised for sale in the magazines.

The possession of a catalogue invariably generates a thirst for more knowledge. If figures are described but not illustrated, what do they look like? If the numbering system in one catalogue does not fit the number on a box in a collection, when did the system change and how often? Some manufacturers seemed to have a new list of numbers each year.

Another advantage of catalogues, particularly illustrated ones, is the opportunity they offer of identifying figures that were previously of unknown manufacture. Particularly satisfying was the recent discovery by Andrew Rose of a Philip Segal catalogue of 1947 in the possession of the son of the original proprietor. In due course this has been reprinted and distributed to collectors, and I was able to identify 27 previously unknown figures, including several that I had had when I was nine years old.

Never miss an opportunity to ask current or former toyshop owners, people in the toy trade or previous employees of toy soldier manufacturers if they have any old catalogues. Other collectors will bless you for any information that can be released. At the time of writing, the whole Britains toy soldier collecting fraternity is waiting for the publication of the most intricate catalogue of all, the Britains Factory Records, which contain details of all the sets and figures made from 1932 onwards, including, so it is surmised, moulding, head and arm casting numbers and painting instructions. Donald Pudney, the enterprising Bermudian collector who acquired these records from Britains, has been preparing them for publication for some years.

COLLECTING BRITAINS BY CATALOGUE

To take as an example of catalogue collecting the most popular toy soldiers – Britains – the most obvious way forward might seem to be the assembly of one of each number in the main military, best quality set numbering series. This would theoretically involve 1,407 boxed sets, not counting sets added after 1960. It would certainly be possible to make an immediate start upon such a collection, but it might be impossible to complete. Britains set numbering included in sequence a considerable number of sets that were produced either for very short periods or in limited numbers for special customers, and even some that were never issued. Many numbers seem never to have been included in a catalogue, which would act as a limit on the collection and reduce the 1,407 sets to about 970.

Even so, acquiring all the display sets with large quantities of figures in each would prove a daunting task, and other areas of near impossibility can soon be detected (see Chapter 12, page 133). Eliminating the display and parade sets that usually merely duplicate figures on offer in single row sets brings a complete Britains collection down to more manageable proportions, and this can then be organized by subject along the lines outlined in Chapter 6. Within each subject area, the depth of collecting that can be achieved is considerable, since there are many versions, variations and different packagings that can be collected (see The Welch Fusiliers, pages 100–1).

COLLECTING BY POINT OF INTEREST

Some of the most interesting collections are those that take an unusual theme and follow it through to a satisfying conclusion. Here are two examples – a collection of castings and a collection of individual figures – taken, as usual, from Britains toy soldiers.

Britains used to sell unpainted castings to collectors, either direct or through Hamleys of Regent Street, which kept a vast stock. In addition, at the end of production in 1966 Britains disposed of an enormous quantity, perhaps half a million figures, to Bill Pierce and Jim Luck acting in consortium, who proceeded to sell them to collectors. I myself bought over a thousand at the time. Before painting, Britains castings show clearly all the fine detail that goes into the moulding, and they could be considered more aesthetically pleasing than the fully painted product. Furthermore, the changes in the moulds that tend to pass unnoticed with painted figures show up much more clearly in the castings.

Britains *set 1527*, the Band of the Royal Air Force. A similar set with its original box fetched £550 at Phillips in 1987 (I). *Phillips*

A collection of castings would be a collection of heads, bodies and arms, all of which could be fitted together to make any figure that Britains produced (as well as many that were never made). It would provide an interesting insight into the on-going design of new figures at Britains, as well as endless ideas for converting battered figures. It would also form the basis of research into the seemingly endless range of variations to be found within the main versions of each set, and become a library of the wording to be found under the base of the figures and the belly of the horses.

Because such a collection need not take into account all the different paint variations for various sets, but simply provide the basic bodies onto which various heads were fitted, it need not be an inordinately large affair. Moreover, since paint condition is immaterial, it would be a relatively cheap project. The idea would be to remove carefully all the paint from those figures that could not be obtained as original castings.

A collection of as many individual figures as possible would be a rather more ambitious and expensive project, and the aim would be to have them in original paint and in good condition. John Tunstill was engaged in this project for many years. However, it has the disadvantage that occasionally it is easier to buy a complete set in order to obtain examples of an officer and a man, when it seems rather wasteful to break up the set. Limiting acquisitions to those opportunities when single figures only may be had would at least enable costs to be kept relatively low.

Collections of individual figures are particularly useful when demonstrating uniforms and versions, as sets need not be disturbed. My own collection has still not been properly sorted back into the sets from which examples were taken for the identification pictures in my last two books. The "one example of each" collection is quite a popular idea among collectors, not only among collectors of Britains figures. Norman Joplin has amassed over 7,000 unduplicated hollow-cast figures, both military and civilian, and Barrie Blood has a collection of over 18,000 unduplicated plastic figures.

THE HAPPY ACCIDENT

While one can always hope, the likelihood is that, whatever collecting plan is undertaken, not everything will prove possible to complete. There is a great deal, therefore, to be said for following up any "happy accident" that may from time to time give the opportunity of acquiring something that has the right associations, appearance or attributes to form the core of an interesting exhibit.

I was lucky enough to have this happen to me. As a boy I lived for some time with my grandmother in Kensington, and our local post office had a small toy department, which at one time had had the benefit of an order from Britains. The post office certainly did not order regularly, because the stock never changed, and I do not think that many people, apart from my friend Jeremy and myself, ever bought anything. It had about half a dozen boxes and two displays of picture packs of the sort that small

An example of the "happy accident" occurred recently when I was walking through Grey's Mews in London and looking at the display on Paul Collet's stall of toy soldiers. I noticed the advertising gimmick distributed by Walpamur to promote its range of enamel paints. It was, presumably, a give-away for dealers or salesmen for the box (**A**) clearly states: "with the compliments of the Walpamur Co. Ltd." Interestingly, the method of achieving the desired painting with only four tins of paint was to supply the plastic figures already dipped in gold and to give instructions for mixing pink flesh colour and light green for the bases, the only additional colour mixes needed.

The boxed set (lower right) is identified on the box (**A**) as the "Monarch" series by John Hill & Co. of Burnley, which usually used the trademark Johillco. Plastic figures by this company are rare, and not only did I already possess these figures, which allowed me to identify the source from which Walpamur obtained its soldiers, but I had also the equivalent figures previously produced by Hill as hollow-cast metal figures (**d**) (lower left). The box (lower right) also carries the additional information that the figures were designed by "Erik", a name I have not come across elsewhere. It took 15 years for the "happy accident" to allow me to connect the promotional box with the other items to form this interesting cameo of one set design in three different applications. *Author's collection*

retailers sometimes ordered so that they could sell the individual figures out of the display rather than, as Britains had intended, having a back up stock as well. At the age of eight, I would ponder these displays and wonder whether I could afford 1s 4½d (7 new pence) for a single Britains figure or the three figures that I could buy for the same money by another manufacturer. Three for the price of one usually won.

When, 10 years later, I heard that the post office was closing down, I dashed over just in case, and those two Picture Pack displays were there, still with half their contents intact. I bought them for half the original retail price of the contents and then proceeded to gut the displays of their compartments, so that I could display other things in them. Later on, of course, when I appreciated original boxes more, I regretted this, but at that time boxes were not often sought after, and virtually all collectors could tell similar tales. Shamus Wade recalls how he and Peter Flateau once stuffed a broken up *box 131* into a convenient dustbin after an auction, because it was too big to fit into their car.

In spite of my vandalism, I now had an interesting nucleus of Picture Pack figures, sufficient to alert me to further chances. Ten more years passed, and I was visiting Brighton, where a militaria shop was divesting itself of a quantity of Britains. I spotted some familiar red-covered cases on the top of a tall cabinet, and, on enquiring, was told that they were of no account since they were empty but, since I had bought a considerable amount, I was quite welcome to them if I wanted them. At home, I found I had acquired a complete set of four Picture Pack displays, so I filled them up as much as I could there and then, and spent another five years completing the contents. Some of the items in the displays are duplicated and *three* mounted Gordon Highlander officers are needed, but eventually they were completed. All I needed then for a complete collection of

Picture Packs were the individual boxes for the figures in the display, and the Picture Pack figures that were only issued in 1954, before the displays were produced. I still do not have them all, but without two happy accidents of collecting I would not have this highlight of my collection. Not only is it an interesting aspect of Britains marketing during the 1950s, it has special memories from my youth and provides excellent examples of the best post-war figures, including some not available elsewhere.

The lesson to be learned, then, is to attune the mind to the most pleasurable collecting memories and to build on them diligently to arrive at a centrepiece that is not likely to feature in many collections.

DISPLAY IDEAS

Possibly the most popular display idea is the coronation procession, and I shall use this as an exhaustive example of a display and follow it up with a list of other ideas that could be carried out along similar lines.

A coronation brings out the acme of royal pageantry and is the most spectacular of all affirmations of national unity and traditions, perhaps best exemplified by those of the British royal family. Because of the large numbers of troops involved, making a model of such an event would be prohibitively expensive, but with toys an appealing and patriotic display is easy to put together.

The nucleus of this display is the state coach, which, since it is the setting in which most ordinary people see the monarch on coronation day, is symbolic of the occasion. As such, it has been extensively offered as a souvenir by toy makers. Various scales are available, from the 5mm scale miniatures by Lesney and Benbros to the 60mm scale item by Timpo.

Coronation coaches are thus generally very common, and millions were sold and proudly preserved on mantlepieces or in china cabinets. Collecting all the different varieties is interesting, and can form a substantial collection in its own right, particularly if the boxes and variations of packing are collected as well. There are some appallingly difficult rarities to collect, such as the Edward VIII coach (see below). This collection can be extended into other souvenirs made by the toy soldier manufacturers, such as individual figures of monarchs, coronation chairs, royal attendants, busts and so on. Few souvenirs in the toy soldier line were made for the 1903 or 1910 coronations, but both 1937 and 1953 saw a liberal supply of models.

Britains produced an extensive range for both 1937 and 1953, starting with the rarest item of all – the state coach made in anticipation of the coronation of Edward VIII before his abdication. Since he was unmarried at the time, the coach contained a single male figure, and examples of the standard Britains state coach, *set 1470*, containing this single figure are extremely scarce. As soon as George VI, married to Elizabeth (now the Queen Mother), was known to be acceding to the throne, a casting of a pair of figures was substituted in the coach, and this model remained

current from 1937 until 1953. The harnessing wire was changed to three die-cast and wire clips about 1949. On the accession of Queen Elizabeth II, the figures in the coach were changed so that the female figure carried the royal regalia, most noticeably the sceptre. About 1959 was started the practice of painting the coach with blue side panels rather than the overall gold finish it had had until then. This gives altogether five variations of the coach that could be collected.

In addition, Britains produced busts of Queen Victoria, Edward VII and Queen Alexandra, George V and Queen Mary (these are very rare), figures of Edward VIII (extremely rare), George VI and Queen Elizabeth (now the Queen Mother) in coronation robes, in painted, gilt or copper finish, miniature state coaches with two, four or eight horses, the latter with two harness variations, the coronation chair and a souvenir stick pin in the form of a crown.

The idea that people might like to put on their own model coronation procession by no means escaped Britains, and most of its new lines in toy soldiers for the year 1937 were aimed at this market. Perhaps the most ambitious coronation project of all would be a complete representation of the procession, keeping strictly to items produced at the time. The list would be: *set 1*, 1st Life Guards (5 figures × 11 boxes = 44 figures + 11 officers), *set 2*, Royal Horse Guards (5 figures × 11 boxes = 44 figures + 11 officers), *set 1477*, 7 Life Guards, 7 Horse Guards, state coach, 18 attendants, 9 infantry at the present with officer, 13 Coldstream Guards at the present with officer, 2 general officers, 2 aides de camp and 4 mounted police. This would make up the nucleus of the procession with the coach, and the two guards each of 24 troopers of the Life Guards to

Britains set *2094*, the State Landau with its escort of Life Guards, Horse Guards and royal attendants (**G**). The second pair of team horses has been incorrectly assembled with the mounted horse on the right. *Phillips*

precede it and the two guards each of 24 troopers of the Horse Guards to follow it.

Britains made Territorial Infantry in blue and green uniforms, New Zealand Infantry and Australian Infantry, all both marching and at the present to feature in the procession. These are sets *1537, 1538* and *1540* to *1545*. Apart from the marching Australians and New Zealanders, they are extremely rare sets, so that to collect any number of them would be quite a feat. *Set 1510*, the marching sailors, on the other hand, is common. Almost equally rare are the Regiments of the British Army series, *sets 1556* to *1602*, which might also be assumed to have taken part in the procession.

After this could be added as many as were wanted of Foot Guard sets, cavalry, Empire contingents, the mounted band of the Life Guards (*set 101*), and Foot Guards, Marine and Line Infantry at the present to line the route, as well as police, mounted and on foot, taking care to include only figures whose paintwork showed them to be of the right parish and which had lightly painted cheeks and thin, neat moustaches.

The 1953 coronation would provide a rather different list. The heart of the collection this time would be the very rare *set 2081*, which contains 181 pieces including the full coach with attendants, the guards of Life Guards and Horse Guards, Irish Guards and Marines at the present and the sovereign's standard and escort. If this set is unobtainable, its component parts may be made up of multiple purchases of *sets 1, 2, 1470, 1475, 2067, 2071* and *2078*.

Other sets made for this coronation were *2072* (the King's Royal Rifle Corps), *2073* (R.A.F. marching), *2074* (1st King's Dragoon Guards), *2075* (7th Queen's Own Hussars), *2076* (12th Royal Lancers), *2077* (King's Troop, Royal Horse Artillery at the walk), *2080* (sailors marching at the slope), *2088* (Duke of Cornwall's Light Infantry at the trail), *2089* (Gloucestershire Regiment at the slope), *2091* (Rifle Brigade at the trail), *2092* (Parachute Regiment at the slope) and *2093* (the Band of the Royal Berkshire Regiment). Some of these sets did not appear until 1954. Once more, sets in the 1953 catalogue would provide more troops and bands to parade with the sets above.

Britains made, as a special commission for the City of Edinburgh, an extremely large model of the 1953 coronation procession, which moved mechanically on an endless belt, returning out of sight underneath the exhibit. The whole display was 36ft (11m) long and was composed of figures, marching eight abreast, soldered onto metal slats. It was subsequently shown in the window of Lyons Corner House, Marble Arch, London, where, to my enormous delight, I saw it when I was 10 years old. Much later, it was broken up, and the figures were distributed among collectors. Many of the figures in this procession were specially cast and painted by Britains, although the most common are the 1910 marching figure with the peaked cap used in the catalogue for the Gloucestershire Regiment. These were painted by Britains with multi-coloured facings and belts to represent all kinds of line regiments and auxiliary services.

Apart from coronation processions, all sorts of parades provide opportunities to display toy soldiers. Some of the more famous events are Trooping the Colour, Changing the Guard, the Royal Tournament, the Edinburgh Tattoo, the Delhi Durbar, the Tidworth Tattoo and the Aldershot Army Display. It is perfectly in order to mount parades or tattoos based entirely on the imagination. Guests at tattoos often include foreign armies and other services, so there is licence to include virtually any toy soldiers. Often, too, there may be room for spectators, in the form of Britains and other hollow-cast civilian figures, watching the parade from a vantage point.

ASSOCIATED COLLECTING IDEAS

Areas of collecting that came close to toy soldiers provide many items that are pleasant to include in displays to add points of interest. Military miniatures, or models, are often collected by toy soldier collectors, although they tend not to look good on the same shelf. Uniforms and equipment, on the other hand, make very good backdrop items for display if there is the room. Buttons and badges can be interesting, and pictures of all sorts, from cigarette cards and postcards to prints and oil paintings, provide a suitable atmosphere.

Vehicles to accompany toy soldiers can form a collection in themselves, and they come in just as wide a variety, including a substantial number of die-cast model cars. Seen here are: (back left) a typical Russian-made missile carrier (**A**); (back centre) a French Renault tank, marked underneath *Mimic Toys* (**B**) – a good name since it mimics "Minic" and the model is a copy of a Rivolet vehicle; (back right) a tinplate tank (**D**) produced as a novelty biscuit tin – the biscuits are reached by taking off the turret; (centre) a six-wheeled early U.S.-made, "slush cast" lead anti-aircraft vehicle equipped with both gun and searchlight (**B**); (front left) a rubber gun carrier, made by the Auburn Rubber Co., U.S.A. (**A**); (front centre) a nice model of the Honey or Stuart M 2 light tank (**B**), probably by Dale of Illinois; (front right) an Honest John missile launcher made by Techno of Denmark (**B**); and (front) an aluminium motorcyclist from France (**A**). *Author's collection*

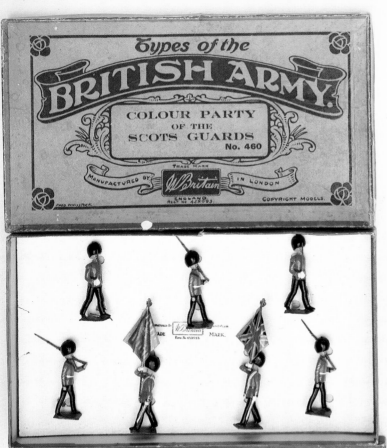

8
CAMEO COLLECTIONS

My favourite idea for collecting is to put together a group of figures that tell a story. I call this a cameo collection. In a way, it is an art form, in that it presents a viewpoint of the collector for consideration by an audience, a single assimilable idea to interest the observer.

A cameo collection makes a statement, but it can be simple or highly decorative according to the taste of the collector. Furthermore, the statement can be about any subject at all – an aspect of history, commercial practice, personal nostalgia or just exceptionally beautiful figures. The trick is to concentrate on the single theme without distraction, although there is nothing to prevent the theme containing hundreds of soldiers. I put this idea into practice at the London Toy and Model Museum in 1985, when the six free-standing cabinets that held about half of my "On Guard" exhibition of toy soldiers, contained a selection of 36 cameos, one on each shelf.

For the Britains collector, a cameo collection could be any one of almost limitless groupings within or across the subject areas listed on page 72. My own especial preferences are: the Balkan Wars, the Boer War, Canada, Italy, Latin America, the Royal Welch Fusiliers, the Royal Scots Greys, the X series, World War II air raid precautions, post-World War II Paris Office figures, Germanic figures and souvenir figures.

The principles of cameo collecting can be applied across the range of manufacturers or any speciality. In cameo, the collection showing different manufacturing methods could comprise just one figure for each method and represent the epitome of that art.

To explain the principles more clearly, I will look at the first example mentioned above – the Balkan Wars – before commenting more briefly on the others.

THE BALKAN WARS

The Balkan Wars, which started in 1911, embroiled Greece, Bulgaria, Montenegro, Serbia, Austria-Hungary and Italy in a war with Turkey. Historically, the wars were part of the struggle for national freedom from the Turks that had been continuing throughout the expansion and decline of the Turkish Empire over several centuries. Britains, in common with Mignot, Heyde, Haffner and others (including many flat figure makers), produced sets of toy soldiers depicting the combatants. The Britains figures were in a series of sets from *165* to *178*, except for

Britains issued only four colour parties as individual sets: set *460*, the Scots Guards (**H**); set *2101*, the U.S. Marines (**H**); set *2111*, the Black Watch (**I**); and set *2171*, the Royal Air Force (**J**). These four sets would make a complete cameo collection, although it would be difficult to complete since the R.A.F. set, even though it had a catalogue number, was never in a catalogue and was almost certainly not widely distributed. It is reputed, for instance, that only two sets were delivered to Canada, and only two sets have ever been on offer at auction in 19 years.

This cameo can be extended by including the special set for Hamleys of the Royal Marines Colour Party (**K**) (lower right) and the re-issue of the Scots Guards colour party as set *2084* with different contents and, later, a change of flags from the tinplate to the cast metal type. It could also include the various other colours and standards made by Britains: set *2067*, the Sovereign's Standard of the Life Guards and escort; the Salvation Army colour bearers (three versions); the colour bearers of the Scots Guards with the pole over the shoulder (three versions); the similar colour bearers of the Royal Welch Fusiliers from set *73*; the Worcestershire Regiment from set *131*; and the Green Howards from set *255*.

I have also seen a Paris Office Italian colour bearer based on the early Salvation Army colour, and there may well be more. If not all of the available figures have been collected, it is always possible to present the cameo differently: sets *460* and *2111*, for instance, would comprise a complete collection of Britains colour parties of the British Army, and sets *460*, *2171* and the Royal Marines would be a "Three Services" display. *Author's collection*

the Turkish cavalry set, which had already been produced as *set 71*. The sets were: Turkey – *set 71*, cavalry (two versions) and *set 167*, infantry (two versions); Italy – *set 165*, cavalry (two versions), *set 168*, infantry (two versions) and *set 169*, Bersagliere (three versions); Greece – *set 170*, cavalry (two versions) and *set 171*, infantry (two versions); Bulgaria – *set 172*, infantry (two versions); Serbia – *set 173*, infantry (two versions); Montenegro – *set 174*, infantry (two versions); and Austria-Hungary – *set 175*, lancers (two versions), *set 176*, dragoons (two versions), *set 177*, infantry of the line (two versions) and *set 178*, Foot Guards (two versions). This gave a total of 14 sets comprising 97 figures.

The smallest complete collection that could be made out of the above would be one soldier from each country – i.e., seven figures – and if this could be arranged so that each would be a different type of figure, there would be an added interest. Unfortunately, the Bulgarian and Montenegrin infantry are both based on the Russian infantry casting, so one of the very rare variations based on the Slade Wallace equipment figure would need to be included to achieve this extra point.

The next larger collection might be one figure from each set; the next would be one of each of the different figures in each set, including officers and trumpeters. After this there would be the achievement of full sets of each, the most exacting form of which would be the collection of dated first versions of each set in their original boxes. As the European sets of Britains are rare and popular among collectors, the purchase of such a collection of 14 sets, if the components were on offer at auction, would probably cost (in 1987) between £7,000 and £10,000.

The collection could then be expanded with the undated second and, where applicable, third versions of each set. The only set to have a third version here is *set 169*, the Bersagliere, which was still in production after World War II. Further linked sets would be the additional sets brought out later for Italy (Abyssinian War) and Greece (Evzones). By this time, with nearly 200 figures, the collection is becoming rather too large and complex to fit the cameo concept.

Yet other cameos could be derived from the Balkan War collection. For instance, a cameo of Greek soldiers would include the two versions of Greek cavalry (an extremely rare possession for any collector), a series of the running Greek infantry, if possible including the rare, open-elbow variation (though I have yet to see an example of this to prove that it exists), and examples of the red jacketed and blue jacketed Evzones, both of which are comparatively common. In boxed set terms, another extremely rare item for the Greek cameo is *set 2176*, which contained four blue Evzones in a "half box" with a Regiments of All Nations colour label.

THE BOER WAR

Britains brought out seven sets of British troops around the time of the Boer War to represent the regiments sent out to South Africa. For many collectors these and other associated items are the most desirable figures

The nucleus of a cameo collection may be made by limiting the subject to drum and fife bands. Britains made only three regular sets of these: *set 321*, Infantry of the Line (J); *set 322*, the Coldstream Guards (J); and *set 2108*, the Welsh Guards (I). Illustrated here are the first two sets mentioned above as well as the eight marching men included in *set 322* (left). To the right at the front is a different version of *set 321* with adult fifers. To the rear is a special painting set of fifes and drums of the Royal Welch Fusiliers (J), originally from the Poitier-Smith collection.

To assemble a larger cameo, conversions of Britains could be included, or bands from other makers could be collected. The history of such bands in the British and foreign armies could be researched to provide background information, and a collector with an interest in delving deep into the recesses of Britains production might research the incidence of boy fifers compared with adult fifers, and when and why the one or the other was included in these sets and as single figures in the other bands. *Author's collection*

This collection of 48mm scale German-made solid figures by Heyde, Haffner and others, depicts the Balkan Wars, when the Balkan States were in conflict with Turkey. Note the moulded lead blobs of fire and smoke at the end of the firing rifles. These figures were being sold for between £10 and £20 each at Phillips in 1987 (h). *Phillips*

The opponents in the Boer War – Imperial Yeomanry (**I**) and Boer Cavalry (**J**) – in their original boxes. They were manufactured by Britains about 1900. *Author's collection*

Britains set *1436*, Italian Infantry in Colonial Service Dress (**I, j**). This was one of the sets issued to portray the Italian invasion of Abyssinia in 1936. *Sotheby's*

of all. First versions of these sets in their original boxes, in good condition, are generally extremely rare and command prices from £300 to over £1,000. There are seven sets.

Set 104, the City Imperial Volunteers on guard in slouch hats, officer with sword and pistol, had the distinction of being the first set to be first issued with a date on the base of the figure. It could thus form a cameo in its own right.

Set 105, the Imperial Yeomanry, fixed arm cavalry figures with slouch hats, is a companion to *set 104*, the two sets together thus forming another cameo.

Set 108, the 6th Dragoons, were the same figures as in *set 105* but with the heads changed to smooth, foreign-service helmets.

Set 109, the Dublin Fusiliers, was of new figures marching at the trail, with Slade Wallace equipment and, in its first version, with smooth, foreign-service helmets.

Set 110, the Devonshire Regiment, comprised the same figures as in *set 109*, but with arms at the slope. The coat and trousers of this figure were always painted the same khaki, while the trousers of *set 109* were always painted a lighter cream colour as opposed to the dark khaki jacket.

Set 114, the Cameron Highlanders, contained new marching figures with Slade Wallace equipment and kilts, again, in the rare first version, wearing the smooth, foreign-service helmets.

Set 119, the Gloucestershire Regiment, standing firing, were wearing

A cameo collection formed of Latin American soldiers could include the seven early sets made by Britains and seen here. From left to right: *set 220*, Uruguayan Cavalry (**H**); *set 222*, Uruguayan Infantry (**H**); *set 221*, Uruguayan Cadets (**H**); *set 186*, Mexican Infantry (**H**); *set 219*, Argentine Cadets (**I**); *set 216*, Argentine Infantry (**G**); and *set 217*, Argentine Cavalry (**H**). *Author's collection*

foreign-service helmets with puggarees and puttees, as opposed to the normal firing figures which were equipped with gaiters.

Associated sets were *set 6*, Boer Cavalry, *set 26*, Boer Infantry (of which there were several versions) and *set 38*, which is South African Mounted Infantry (unless you have the box that titles it Dr Jameson and the African Mounted Infantry). One small size *set 126*, the Royal Artillery in foreign service dress, was made for the Boer War period, and the Cameron Highlanders, *set 23B*, and the second version of the 16th Lancers, *set 12B*, also fit in nicely.

CANADA

Canada is also one of my Britains subjects, number 17 on page 72, but some areas are sufficiently small to make good cameos, and this is one of them (the others being the Boer War, France, Latin America, historical, American Civil War, cowboys and Indians, buildings and Picture Packs). Canadian forces were the subject of 13 regular sets of Britains, three double-row sets and a number of Picture and souvenir Packs based on the Royal Canadian Mounted Police and Fort Henry Guard.

ITALY

Apart from the early three sets of Italian troops, three more sets were produced for the Abyssinian War of 1936, together with two sets of Abyssinians. One might also include in an Italian cameo the Papal State Swiss Guard, *set 2022*.

Britains set *1837, Infanteria Argentinea con Casco* (Argentine infantry in steel helmets), was issued in 1939 (**J, k**). *Sotheby's*

LATIN AMERICA

A convenient cameo, Latin America can also include the Mexicans, which were the first set produced. These were followed by a group of sets probably designed for export to Argentina and Uruguay, including cavalry, infantry and cadets of both countries, together with cavalry and a new version of infantry for Spain, the mother country. These eight sets were produced in 1925. A further small and rare group of sets came out in 1939. It was composed of Argentine infantry in steel helmets, military and naval cadets. A large number of double- and triple-row sets was also issued, probably solely for export to the Argentine. After World War II, Venezuelan infantry, sailors and cadets were issued, again with some display boxes, and the cameo is completed with a new version of the Uruguayan cadets, *set 2051*.

THE ROYAL WELCH FUSILIERS

As I have mentioned earlier, the Royal Welch Fusiliers is my favourite infantry regiment, and it is, in itself, more a whole collection than just a cameo. Several cameos may, however, be derived from it. I have taken this regiment, a box of which were my first best quality Britains, and expanded it as far as is reasonably possible. When they were first bought for me, I was intrigued by their crossbelts and pack – indeed they were the only British regiment made by Britains after World War II to retain a pack in full dress. When I got them home and discovered that I could move the arms at the slope to a good-enough equivalent of on guard, I was ecstatic. The six men formed a hedge of broad bladed bayonets, and my former favourites, the second-grade infantry of the line, were instantly demoted to enemy troops (Germans, because of the spiked helmets).

Since that time, on every level of collecting, I have found an intellectual interest in collecting the Fusiliers. *Set 74* has, throughout Britains' sales history, been a popular set. It was introduced in 1897 and had an uninterrupted sale until 1965.

The first cameo is to show how the officers and men changed from the early valise-pack figure of 1897 to the figures I had bought for me in 1950. The first version of the Welch Fusiliers was the valise-pack marching figure of 1897 with fixed bayonet at the slope on a movable arm. This was an oval-base figure, with no mark underneath. The set comprised a fixed arm, bemedalled officer, a goat and seven men and was rather better than the normal value of eight figures to a set; soon after, however, the goat counted as a figure and only six men were included.

The first change to the set was when a movable arm, wasp-waisted officer was put in. Then, in 1905, both the men and officer changed to new, dated figures, the men dated 1.8.1905 and the officer dated 16.11.1905. About 1908, these figures, still dated, were changed to the square base, so that the oval-base version of the dated figure is quite rare.

The square-base figure with gaiters continued from 1908 through to about 1935, but during this time both the head and the rifle arm were improved, the head becoming a little larger and with a plume moulded in the right side, and the arm changing from one with a loose sling hanging in a loop to a flattish rifle with a taut sling, and then, about 1930, to a square, cross section rifle. In 1935, the legs were remodelled to show a full trouser; in 1939, moustaches ceased to be painted on the figures; and in 1949 yet another rifle was introduced, this one with the broad bladed bayonet. About 1935 the officer, who had carried a sword since 1897, was also given full trousers and ceased to carry the sword. Although these are the main changes to be observed, keen-eyed collectors often point out to me more minor variations in the moulds.

I have assembled a *set 74* showing each of the above versions, but also thought it would be fun to march a complete battalion down a display, each company being a different version. For each company there are four platoons of 16 men with 4 officers, pioneers or colour bearers, so that a full strength company is 80 men. In order to fill out the ranks at low cost, I have included all conditions, repaired and even re-cast figures, so that at the moment there is a big repair and repainting job waiting for whenever I have the time. In addition to the various marching versions, I decided to see what the Fusiliers would look like at all the other drill positions that Britains made, so I have platoons to be made up at attention, at ease, at the present, on guard (standing and kneeling), standing, kneeling and lying firing, running at the trail, marching without packs and in greatcoats, as well as a number of bands — all to be completed as if Britains had originally made them. The 1st Battalion wears gaiters; the 2nd Battalion is in full trousers. There are also a number of Fusiliers by new toy soldier manufacturers included to add variety to the display, which at present contains about 1,100 figures.

THE ROYAL SCOTS GREYS

The Royal Scots Greys occupy a similar place in my collection for cavalry as the Royal Welch Fusiliers do for the infantry. There was a much larger variety of sets containing the Scots Greys than there was with the Welch Fusiliers, and it is possible to have a complete cameo showing the six sets that Britains produced in best quality. The sets were: *set 32*, the standard, five figure cavalry box; *set 59*, a similar set, but with 10 figures; *set 1720*, a seven-piece mounted band; *set 1721*, a 12-piece mounted band; *set 2119*, a small set containing a mounted officer and two dismounted troopers; and *set 6B*, a small size set containing four troopers in 45mm scale. The Scots Greys were the most popular cavalry regiment after the Household Cavalry, and Britains included them in a large number of large boxes. I particularly like the large display box *73*, because it contains both the Scots Greys and Welch Fusiliers, with the added bonus for the Fusiliers of offering a colour bearer and two pioneers.

THE X SERIES

Since there is no known list of what was in the X series of Britains second-grade figures, this cameo collection is of particular interest to the research-minded collector. I have cavalry boxes with labels stating 4x 1st

Britains made two sets of the Royal Engineers in full dress: *203*, the Pontoon section (**I**), and *1330*, the General Service Limbered Waggon. The early pontoon waggon, shown at the back (**J**), came with a team of collar harness horses. The two pieces of planking and the canvas rolls that formed the roadway for each boat are missing, as is the boat on the waggon on the left. The limbered waggon sometimes came with walking horses, sometimes with galloping horses. Both the examples shown are post-World War II productions (**I**). They show the Royal Engineers in full dress with red jackets and spiked helmets.

At the extreme left is a group of Britains specials showing the Royal Engineers in the new full dress of the busby with blue bag: a limbered waggon, officer and five mounted men (**K**). To the right is a different group of special figures in spiked helmets, nine marching on foot with officer, two officers on round bases and three mounted figures (**J**). These are specials from the large collection assembled by L. Poitier-Smith in the late 1930s, and the painting detail is of a superior standard to the normal toys. *Author's collection*

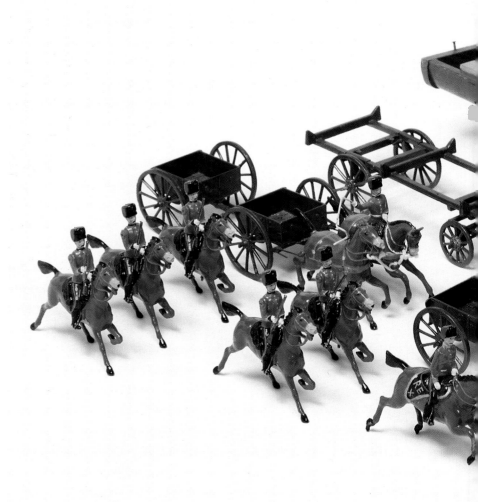

Dragoons, and 8x 6th Dragoon Guards, but they do not bear Britains trade mark, although the fixed arm figures that they contain are certainly by Britains. Similar infantry boxes have turned up for the Somerset Light Infantry and the Worcestershire Regiment, but this time without any X series reference number on the box. Other early second-grade figures that are thought to have been included in the X series are the East Kent Regiment, Life Guards, Horse Guards, Scots Greys, 3rd Hussars, 12th Lancers, North American Indians crawling, cowboys, Zulus, Boy Scouts, Royal Marines, Black Watch and West Surrey Regiment. All these need to have definite reference numbers before their inclusion in the X series is certain, and research is also needed to determine when Britains first

issued second-grade sets, when (since some boxes have no reference numbers) they were referred to as the X series, and at what date (possibly in the 1920s) the X series ceased and the A series began.

WORLD WAR II AIR RAID PRECAUTIONS

Although this cameo is great fun, as it includes a number of scenic effects and equipment to make up a tableau, unfortunately most of the constituents are rather rare. The AA instruments, 2–pounder AA gun and searchlight are easy enough to find, but the 4.5in AA gun, air raid precautions anti-gas suited stretcher parties, air raid wardens and associated buildings are decidedly not.

At the rear of this group are Britains extremely rare Air Raid Wardens, *set 1914* (**J, k**). In front is the more common Taylor & Barratt decontamination squad in anti-gas suits (**f**); after the experience of World War I, the threat of chemical warfare was taken very seriously. The stretcher party in anti-gas suits on the right is Britains second-grade paint (**A**). *Sotheby's*

POST-WORLD WAR II PARIS OFFICE FIGURES

This cameo may sound like a contradiction in terms, but it is a fascinating thing to search for and one that I have not yet put together. On closing the Paris Office and factories in 1923, Britains returned all the moulds to London, where they became part of the stock in trade. After World War II, a number of the figures that had hitherto been made only in Paris were brought out of the vaults in order to create some new sets. The three examples that I have particularly identified are the new Life Guard officer at the canter for *set 1*, which has the double date 12.2.1903 & 9.5.1905 on it, and is thus a reworking of the French cavalry officer figure; the French Foreign Legion officer with shoulder boards, which was available only as a picture pack; and the French Foreign Legion charging figure, available as a picture pack and in *set 2095*. There are probably a number of others that I have not noticed, and it would also be interesting to note how many post–World War II figures still have *Déposé* stamped under the base.

GERMANIC FIGURES

This cameo includes all the very earliest Britains figures, which may well have been designed by a German firm for Britains, since they have a remarkable resemblance to the contemporary, solid-cast offerings from Germany. The figures are the early cavalry that did duty in *sets 1, 2* and *3*, the plug-shouldered lancers and Scots Greys, the latter being used also as a mounted Fusilier officer, the plug-handed Fusilier, and the plug-handed Highlander used for *sets 11, 15, 77* and *88*. All these figures are very rare, although the first and the last are less so.

SOUVENIR FIGURES

From time to time Britains produced souvenir figures, most of which were to do with coronations. A collection of these, not going so far as to collect a complete coronation procession (see page 92) would be most interesting, including such rare items as the souvenir figure of Emperor

CAMEO COLLECTIONS

Wilhelm II and the Queen Victoria Diamond Jubilee set of Life Guards 1837 and 1897.

The list of cameo collections that could be made is endless. Apart from my own favourites, you could make one up of the Territorials and Yeomanry depicted by Britains. The earliest part-time volunteers to be made were the Middlesex Yeomanry, *set 83*; then you could include the City Imperial Volunteers, *set 105*, Imperial Yeomanry, *set 105*, Territorial Yeomanry, *set 159*, Territorial Infantry, *set 160*, the Red and the Blue Territorial Troops made for the 1910 coronation at the slope and at ease with mounted officer, the Blue and Green Territorials at the slope, at the present and in walking-out dress made for the 1937 coronation, the militia and the Home Guard.

Another cameo might be to show in how many different scales Britains made toy soldiers. This cameo would be impossible to complete, since the smallest toy soldiers Britains ever made were those presented for Queen Mary's dolls' house at Windsor Castle, and the only other examples are at the Bethnal Green Museum of Childhood and are on loan from Britains. Other scales produced by Britains were: lilliput infantry (plastic, scaled down versions of the Herald Combat Infantry, 20mm scale, 1959); miniature cavalry (30mm scale, 1901); larger miniature cavalry with Edward VII (35mm scale, 1903); early small size B series (43mm scale, 1898); later small size B and W series (45mm scale, 1904); M series cavalry; O gauge civilians (there are no soldiers in exactly this scale); mini-set plastic figures in the 1960s; plug-shoulder lancers (50mm scale); early standard size (52mm scale); A series cavalry (53mm scale); standard size (54mm scale); plug-shoulder fusiliers (62mm scale); Madame Tussaud souvenir figures (65mm scale); H size (70mm scale); experimental cavalry (60mm scale, dated 1907); HH size (83mm scale) racing colours (67mm scale); and souvenir figures of King George VI and Queen Elizabeth (75mm scale).

Although a number of civilian figures have to be included to obtain the whole variety of scales, there are 18 different sizes, more including the various garden ornaments and souvenirs that Britains produced. Another cameo would comprise all the Britains figures that did not fit into a series scale – i.e., excluding small size B and W series, second grade and standard size.

To my mind, building cameos is the most interesting way to present a collection, and a number of them can be linked to tell the history of a manufacturer or whatever it pleases a collector to highlight in his collection. Building a cameo with some new object in mind is even more exciting, exploring the neglected areas of toy soldier collecting, such as cowboys and Indians, Britains second grade, the model piracies in the plastic era, when so many figures were copied both in England and Hong Kong, and building up recognition cameos of the lesser known hollow-cast makers of 1930 to 1960.

Conversions for campaigns.

Illustrated on the top row are ideas for simple head conversions of the Britains Maxim gunner, a very common model (**b**), which is usually to be found in poor condition in everyone's odds and ends box. On the left it has a slouch hat, then a foreign-service helmet, as if in the Boer War. The next figure has had the gun cut away so that he can use his hands to feed an ammunition belt to his colleague. The fourth figure from the left is a copy of Britains, done as a Highlander lying with a machine gun. The last figure is given a wounded head from the Medical Corps set and a red jacket: this seems rather anachronistic to me, but makes a good-looking toy.

On the centre row, the figure on the left is another extremely common second-grade figure (**a**) on guard in battledress. The rifle has been trimmed away, and a shell has been built up out of modelling material, so that, with very little effort, a useful gunner has been created. The second figure is a model of Queen Victoria in mourning, easily achieved from an early Britains nurse. Next is a re-cast, bemedalled Fusilier officer, the colour of the coat a little too orange to be correct. The bugler at attention was created simply by substituting a movable arm. The Foot Guard kneeling on guard is just a head change. Next is a re-cast figure of an early Infantry of the Line in the same pose. Acquiring a large quantity of early Britains figures for a display would be extremely expensive, so re-casting is the only way to achieve this cheaply (**b**). The next figure is a charging Infantry of the Line, a re-cast conversion from a Britains Japanese figure, and next is a re-cast conversion figure of a Highlander on guard.

The Indian Army figure at the right of the centre row and the cavalryman below have been superbly repainted by Freddie Green.

At the left of the bottom row are Argentine copies of Britains Argentine cavalry and infantry (**f**), with an Argentine machine gunner, the gun being a copy of Britains gun and the figure coming from Comet. The Crescent mounted trumpeter, once a Scots Grey, looks much better with a foreign-service helmet, and the Hill Highlander has also been given the foreign-service treatment with a pack. *Author's collection*

9
CAMPAIGNING WITH TOY SOLDIERS

One of the satisfying aspects of toy soldiers, as opposed to some other collectable objects, is the ability to play with them as they were played with – i.e., to take them on campaign. H. G. Wells and his friends in *Little Wars* (1913) were only following other publications by Britains and the Boy Scouts, which had already advocated war-gaming as a pastime, and to do this with the hollow-cast Britains figures is particularly delightful. Today, apart from the devotees of the *Plastic Warrior* (see page 142), not many collectors actually war-game with their troops for fear of breakages, war-gaming having come of age with figures made especially for the purpose. However, to build up a display as if one were going to fight a toy campaign is most enjoyable and involves a much larger collecting plan than for a single subject or cameo. It also gives full scope for the use of all the toy troops in action that cannot easily be fitted into the parade ground displays discussed hitherto.

CHOOSING A CAMPAIGN
Britains collectors tend to choose campaigns between 1879 and World War I involving the British Army. Suitable campaigns would be the Zulu Wars, the north-west frontier of India, the Sudan campaigns, the Boxer Expeditionary force, the Boer War and World War I itself. Other wars during this period included the Spanish–American War, the Sino–Japanese and Russo–Japanese Wars and the Balkan Wars. Choosing a campaign is by no means limited to these, but depends on the sort of toy soldiers that one wishes to collect to form the participants. There are large numbers of reference books available in which to study the history, uniforms and equipment involved.

ASSEMBLING CAMPAIGNERS
Having decided on the campaign, the next step is to plan an order of battle, which may include one or both sides, and be more or less realistic according to taste. While the model soldier collector has to take endless pains to get his research right, the toy soldier buff need not be at all exact, since the representation is only a playful one. Having said that, the impression that is given should be something like the real thing, unless there are special circumstances.

One of the most useful adjuncts to any campaign is a naval brigade, and this can be made up of Britains naval landing party with running blue- and white-jackets, as well as contingents of the marching second-

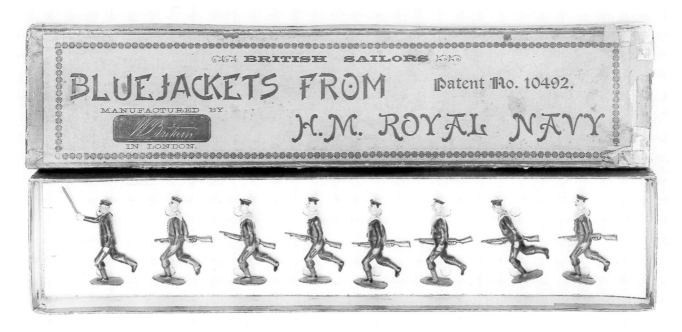

grade blue-jackets in straw hats. In building up a force, the object is to have as many reasonably priced figures as possible, so this is when getting large auction lots of assorted repainted and broken items comes in handy. Many makers of collectors' toy soldiers today also feature naval figures in their lists, so, by taking care to get the ones that best fit in with Britains, a good force can be built up. Next, the models of Hill, Crescent and so on should be examined to see if these cheaper makes have anything to offer. The Hill standing and kneeling on guard Navy figures are very acceptable, requiring little further work than some embellishment to make them fit in with Britains paintwork.

When it comes to infantry, nearly all the British regiments of the line looked similar when on foreign service, so it is just a question of getting hold of sufficient of the basic figures. Here it is perfectly in order to start re-casting figures to put the quantities up, and if you have not got the necessary expertise, there are many people who will be glad to help at a reasonable cost. This is another reason for belonging to a club, because the sort of practical person whose help you need is quite likely to be a member, and talking over your problem will show you the way forward. Here also is the opportunity to do the things that Britains never did, and have, for instance, City Imperial Volunteers standing, kneeling and lying firing, with officers with binoculars, instead of the regular on guard set. To make this, one needs the basic figure in puttees, which is easy for the standing figure, where one can use a Gloucestershire Regiment figure with a head change, but more difficult in the kneeling and lying figure, where one would need to find a spare kneeling and lying U.S. doughboy figure, from set 1251, from which to cast. Infantry for the Zulu campaign are easier, since at that time gaiters were worn, and most of the early Britains infantry were thus equipped.

For Highlanders, it is just a question of assembling sufficient figures and perhaps changing them to the attractive, smooth foreign-service helmet and painting their jackets khaki. I commissioned from Giles Brown of Dorset Metal Model Soldiers some very successful conversion castings of Highlanders standing and kneeling on guard, in smooth foreign-service helmets, to complement the firing figures.

Of course, all the figures in original boxes that Britains produced for each of these campaigns can come and join the fun, but in order to get impressive numbers, repainting, repairing and re-casting are likely to be essential.

Cavalry figures are even harder to come by and are relatively expensive from the new toy soldier manufacturers, since they contain more metal as solid-cast figures, and are much trickier to cast. Britains broken cavalry still cost only about £4 per figure, and the conversion to foreign service dress with most figures is just a change of head.

ARTILLERY AND EQUIPMENT

Any campaigner would be wise to equip himself with plenty of guns, ammunition, baggage and supplies. Here, there is a good variety of

OPPOSITE ABOVE
The change of sword arm for a lance, a new bearded head and a red coat completely transform the appearance of the standard Britains Cossack. Originals are the third, fifth and sixth figures from the left. *Sotheby's*

OPPOSITE CENTRE
Britannia Model Company (B.M.C.) was an outstanding competitor of Britains immediately after World War I, but its figures are rare because of the contemporary distaste for war toys. The sides of this box fall flat to form a base for the model field entrenchment, which is filled with firing troops in khaki and peak caps, representing British infantry as in the British Expeditionary Force in France in 1914 (**E**). *Shire Publications*

OPPOSITE BELOW
Britains set 78, Bluejackets of the Royal Navy, is seen here in its first version with the oval-based officer and the original early box (**H, h**). *Phillips*

A display of early Britains toy soldiers depicting troops on campaign in the Sudan. Britains never made any proper Dervishes, but this lack can be supplied from modern makers of new toy soldiers for the collector (see page 114). The troops shown here are the first and second versions of *sets 117*, Egyptian Infantry (**H**); *116*, Sudanese Infantry (**H**); *48*, Egyptian Camel Corps (**H**); *115*, Egyptian Cavalry (**H**); *94*, 21st Lancers (**I**); with first versions of *set 28*, Mountain Artillery (**H**), and *79*, Naval Landing Party (**H**), and two British Camel Corps from *set 131* (**m**), assorted Arabs and palm trees (**g**). The current (1987) cost of the figures shown here, with appropriate original boxes if there are sets, would be about £4,000 for the 118 figures, if bought at auction in London. *Author's collection*

These Heyde figures of Indian Army cavalry attacking a Burmese village from the Hanington collection sold for £1,100 in 1984. German toy soldier manufacturers showed great imagination in their choice of subject matter (**L**). *Phillips*

Britains Arabs (**f**) and, in the foreground, the rare Eastern People (**i**), are shown on the sort of scenic layout that some collectors prefer as a setting for their figures. The date and coconut palms (**g**) are also by Britains and were cast as flat models. *Phillips*

products from new toy soldier makers, although some of the vehicles are somewhat oversized for my taste. I prefer, as Britains did, to produce vehicles and accessories in a slightly smaller scale than the soldiers. Some items, such as tents and sandbags, can easily be home-made with the aid of a sewing-machine, if original old items cannot be found. Boxes and barrels can be made out of dowelling and light timber.

Britains did not provide any dismounted gunners for its early gun teams, but converting the later *set 313* from peak caps to foreign–service helmets is very satisfactory, and even using the later figures handling shells works equally well. There are also a multitude of quite good toy guns to choose from, my favourite being a re-cast Renvoize gun. With a toy campaign there is no need to have sufficient gun teams and limbers for all the guns, as most of them will probably be in action in any display. One item not to be forgotten in the later campaigns is a good supply of machine guns, and here any of the later Britains' figures can be used, again with an appropriate head change. These figures were prolific and are therefore cheap, and by cutting the machine gun off the lying figure, a good loader can be obtained for the sitting figure.

SCENERY AND ACCESSORIES

I have made it a rule not to introduce into a campaign display any item that cannot be called a toy, largely because to display toy soldiers on a scenic, landscaped background strikes a note of discord. Sometimes I have made an exception in the case of model trees, which sometimes look charmingly toylike, but usually I like to add toy trees and other scenery to the display, including any buildings that may be needed. Landscaping is, to my mind, best done *à la* H. G. Wells, with large wooden blocks, or, more simply, with books covered in thin cloth of a suitable colour.

What scenery there is will be dictated by the room that can be given to the display, of which more in Chapter 10. One good idea for making up buildings is to use construction toys. My favourites are Minibrix and an Italian-made, castle-building toy that is rather like Lego but made in a simulated stone colour. Traditionally, wooden forts have been the proper furniture to go with toy soldiers, but these tend not to fit well into campaigns, and there is no altering their shape to suit. Another solution is to collect old sets of stone bricks, which are still very cheap, and build them up, using thin plywood for floors.

TWO UNUSUAL CAMPAIGNS

A cross between a parade and a campaign is to depict the British Army in the 1890s on manoeuvres in Britain, when full dress was still commonly used. This enables the use of all the Britains action figures such as Foot Guards in bearskins, which are otherwise unusable until as far back as the Crimean War, when the uniforms and equipment were rather different. Re-creating a mock campaign in the English countryside also gives an opportunity for using all Britains farm and garden accessories to decorate the display.

Another favourite of mine is the Boxer Rebellion of 1900, which is the only campaign in which all the major European nations and Japan combined, in an imperialist adventure to relieve the legations in Peking. The Britains troops of the various nations were not created with this event in mind, but I feel that it is legitimate to allow them to go into action together on this occasion in what are evidently the wrong uniforms. At the time, most of the participants wore khaki, but it is a splendid opportunity to show the uniforms of many nations together and also to use a great deal of imagination as to what the Chinese might have worn. Not a few new toy soldier manufacturers have now addressed this subject, and the Boxer figures by Trophy are particularly spectacular.

A rare Britains Japanese cavalry with dark blue coat. It is not yet known why this paint variation was issued, for normally the cavalry and infantry wore light blue coats (**k**). *Sotheby's*

Compared with the illustration on pages 110–11, which shows the figures brought out by Britains at the time of the events depicted, this scene shows Egyptians (right) and Dervishes (left) including conversions and newly created figures for the modern collector. On the Egyptian side, the Britains figures, while still quite recognizable, have mostly been retouched or fully repainted. The green colour of the bases of the Sudanese infantry on the far right, for

example, is obviously far too dark to be original. The Egyptian infantry figures have been provided with a converted officer and standard bearer. Next to the Egyptian infantry is a contingent of dismounted British Camel Corps made by David Bracey, and the Egyptian Camel Corps are led by British Camel Corps figures by Empire Models and Trophy. The Imperial infantry in khaki are supplied in the front rank by re-cast Britains figures and another make, and the two rows

at the rear by Bastion, which also made the gun and crew. To the rear are single examples of Britains 21st Lancers and York and Lancaster Regiment, made for the occasion at the time. The Whitejackets, including the extremely rare Naval Landing Party in white, are original Britains, except for the two figures in straw hats, which are very attractive conversions by Freddie Green.

On the Dervish side many additional

figures are available to add to the Arabs, which were all that Britains provided in the early days. At the rear are mounted Dervishes by Blenheim and Trophy, and a contingent of Arabs on foot by Comet. To the rear of these is a group of Dervishes by Lancer. At the forefront of the Dervish forces are charging figures, mostly converted from Britains Zulus, and behind these (to the left) is a strong force of Dorset "fuzzy wuzzies" equipped with various arms. At the front left, the Britains charging Arabs include some conversions, and these are followed by repainted, marching Abyssinian tribesmen. A sprinkling of the excellent Dervishes made by Trophy and a couple of "fuzzy wuzzies" by Soldiers Soldiers complete the picture. There are just over 300 figures in the tableau, which cost under £1,000 to assemble over a period of 10 years, or well under £10 a month at current (1987) values (**d–g**). *Author's collection*

10
DISPLAY, STORAGE AND TRANSPORT

Although toy soldiers are not individually very large, even a medium-sized collection of some hundreds of figures will take up a certain amount of space. I have worked out a rough rule of thumb that to display soldiers attractively is likely to cost as much as the soldiers themselves.

Collections including packaging will take up far more room than one composed of figures only, the more so since on occasions the soldiers will need to be out of their boxes, and the empty boxes will then still take up just as much room. If you wish to show a fully fledged collection, with the soldiers nicely spread out and their boxes in attendance, you could easily fill a gallery about 25×25ft (7.6×7.6m) with just some 4,000 figures.

Equally space-consuming is any attempt to indulge in layouts, scenic or otherwise. On parade, each standard, 54mm foot soldier takes up about 1 square inch (6.5sq cm) and each cavalry soldier about 3×1in (8×2.5cm). To display soldiers properly, there should be at least as much room between units as the units themselves cover, so 1 square foot (9.3 sq decimetre) will take 72 infantry or 24 cavalry. Vehicles, guns or scenery take up a great deal more space.

Layouts can be done on tabletops or on specially constructed working surfaces. My own ideal is a working surface at table height (30in/76cm from the floor), extending 30–36in (76–90cm) from the wall, with cupboards underneath for boxes and glass shelves to the ceiling over the top. The lowest shelf would be at least 12in (30cm) above the working surface and not more than 12in (30cm) deep. There should be space for four shelves. These shelves can have glazed, sliding doors on runners fixed to the bottom shelf, or wall fittings may be used. Open shelving leaves the soldiers prone to collect harmful dust but is a lot less expensive. Many collectors prefer to fit a whole wall with glazed shelves from top to bottom and this also is very satisfactory, although there is less chance of setting out a large display. Backing shelves with mirrors can give the illusion of greater depth and numbers, but the best effect is achieved if this is used sparingly and the soldiers are displayed marching or moving parallel with the mirror.

One interesting way of displaying figures is to convert a deep picture frame to give an inch or more of shelf space across the frame behind glass. A number of individual soldiers, boxes or sets can then be framed and hung as pictures. Alternatively, frames can be made to fit around boxes and trays, with the set of figures strung in place.

A collector with his collection: Ed Ruby, with possibly the world's finest definitive collection of Britains toy soldiers. His steel-framed glass cabinets are ideal for displaying a large collection.

When exhibiting in a display cabinet, making different patterns with the toys gives a more interesting display. *Author's collection*

As far as scenery is concerned, I prefer to use only toys with a similar degree of verisimilitude as the soldiers. It is possible to create beautifully landscaped, scenic layouts similar to those used with model railways, but I feel that toy soldiers (as opposed to model soldiers) look rather out of place in this type of setting. H. G. Wells had the right idea in *Little Wars* when he recommended that large blocks of wood or old books covered with thin cloth of appropriate colours be used to provide a series of stepped platforms, on which the soldiers will more easily stand than on slopes.

STORAGE

I have always preferred to store my soldiers in cardboard boxes of appropriate size either to contain the original toy soldier boxes or a single layer of figures. Boxes that are too shallow may mean that fragile pieces break off when the lid is closed, and it is as well to allow a little extra depth, as the centres often sag downwards somewhat when heavy boxes are put on top of each other. Cardboard boxes are not expensive to buy from a box maker, and disused shoe-boxes or shirt-boxes can often be begged from the appropriate shop.

LEAD AND LEAD ALLOYS

Lead solid-cast figures and lead alloy hollow-cast figures such as Britains are sometimes prone to a condition known among collectors as "lead disease". This occurs when impurities in the lead cause it to oxydize, often forming lead sulphide or similar compounds, which have a grey, powdery appearance. Various agents are known to heighten the risk of this happening, the major ones being water, either as damp or high humidity, domestic mothballs and the exudation of organic acids by various woods, particularly oak. The more seasoned the wood, the less the risk, but I have seen several examples of collections damaged by storage in oak furniture.

"Lead disease" usually shows itself as a roughish grey that discolours exposed parts of toy soldiers such as bases, bayonets, helmets and breastplates that have not been painted. At first, it is just a loss of shine, and this should not be confused with the dullness of lead that has simply aged with time and handling. "Lead disease" will feel slightly gritty to the touch. Detecting "lead disease" is another good reason for looking under the bases of toy soldiers, since this is usually where it is to be seen first. The advanced stages of "lead disease" are easy to see: the reaction works its way right into the interior of hollow-cast figures, the paint starts to crumble away, the thin parts of the casting are weakened and holes start to appear. A model in this condition can disintegrate completely if it is dropped.

"Lead disease" occurs quite often in figures that have been rescued from storage in a garage or damp cellar. However, if the condition is not far advanced, many collectors are not too worried by it, since removing the conditions under which the reaction takes place halts any further deterioration, and, unlike a real disease, there is no danger of it spreading to other figures. A certain amount of restoration can be attempted, and there are methods of reconstituting the metal chemically although it will never be quite as new. Alternatively, affected areas can be brushed off, repainted and sealed with polyurethane. "Diseased" figures should be somewhat cheaper to buy.

In 30 years of storing figures, I have not yet detected any harmful effects from wrapping them in tissue paper (acid-free paper is preferable) and putting them in cardboard boxes. The main precaution to be followed is not to put the soldiers in too airtight an environment. I once put a number of Zulus into an airtight display case, and they all contracted "lead disease" over the course of the ensuing eight months, although figures on display nearby did not. Wrapping soldiers in plastic of any kind over a long period can have the same effect. Wrapping soldiers in fibrous material such as cotton wool can be harmful as the material gets caught in any minute cracks, or adheres to the paint and can be extremely difficult or damaging to remove.

When cleaning metal soldiers, apart from just brushing off dust, light oil is better than water. Interestingly, one of the best ways of keeping soldiers looking good is to handle them often. The more loving attention they receive, the better off they seem to be, because the microscopic layer of oil secreted by the collector's fingers is deposited on the figures.

HIGH TIN CONTENT FIGURES

Tin is a much more stable metal than lead, and flats and the better modern collector toy figures that are made with a high proportion of tin in the alloy are unlikely to come to harm. The only problem with them is that they can be somewhat brittle when bent, but this, of course, applies to most toy soldiers. When buying new collector figures, it is an added plus to know that the figures have a high proportion of tin, and are thus not susceptible to "lead disease".

DIE-CAST FIGURES

Die-casting was not often used for making toy soldiers themselves, but since the early 1930s it has been extensively used for vehicles and guns. The metal used is a zinc alloy, often known as Mazac after the name of one of the leading commercial suppliers. Early die-castings often suffered from impurities in the alloy, often too much lead, which resulted in a phenomenon that has been dubbed "metal fatigue" among collectors, as the symptom is a maze of tiny cracks forming in the metal over a period of years until, finally, the model collapses into fragments.

Once a figure shows these symptoms, there is no known cure, although a dip in polyurethane can help to keep the pieces together. Modern die-castings, such as the new Britains toy soldiers, should not suffer from this problem, since the alloys are subject to tighter quality controls.

A useful way of detecting fatigue in a die-cast gun barrel is to see if it is at all bent. If the barrel is cast in two halves, sometimes one half has "metal fatigue", and the expansion caused by the cracks causes a bend.

COMPOSITION FIGURES

Once more the chief enemy is damp, as the wire skeleton inside composition figures can rust and the composition itself crack if exposed to too much water. Cracks or breakages can be repaired with plastic wood or Polyfilla, but the figures will never be the same again.

PLASTIC

Contrary to the claims of many manufacturers, plastic soldiers are not unbreakable. In normal play, they become unpleasantly dirty, pitted, bent and paintless in a rather shorter time than hollow-cast toys become scratched, headless, bent and crushed. Particularly in the early days, plastic was a highly experimental substance, and very little of it has yet had to stand the test of time for more than 40 years. The two main types from which toy soldiers are made are the Alkathene/Polythene group and the Polystyrene group.

Polythene gives good "bendability", but it is difficult to paint satisfactorily. Polystyrene is very brittle, and so bayonets and other fragile pieces are liable to break off. For some time it was commercial practice for Herald, Timpo and Lone Star to mix chalk with Alkathene to give better paint adhesion. After some time, the chalk content causes the models to dry out and become very fragile. Particularly in the warm climates of such areas as California and parts of Australia with low humidity, Britains "Eyes Right" figures can become very easily damaged, even just by trying to twist the heads. Some of the accessories made out of soft plastic have a disconcerting habit of melting rather messily. I have some early plastic toy soldiers that are in the process of reverting to a sort of goo. Undoubtedly most plastic figures are perfectly stable, but it is wise to treat them with just as much care as anything else.

PAINTWORK AND PRINTED MATERIAL

The main enemy here is light, particularly sunlight, in which there is a high ultraviolet content, which will quite quickly fade paintwork or printing inks. Avoid exposing soldiers or boxes if at all possible. Paintwork or boxes are best cleaned only with a stiff sable hair brush to remove the dust. Any strong action taken against dirt on paint is just as likely to take the paint off with it. Learning how to clean and restore paint is best done with not very valuable figures. My own inclination is usually to leave things alone. Paintwork on plastic models is particularly liable to flake off, especially if the figure is flexed in any way. Minimum handling is the only solution. Even wrapping figures up will take some paint off flexible figures, and although hard plastic figures take the paint much better, they are more brittle in themselves.

All toy soldiers, therefore, should be stored in covered cardboard boxes, with or without tissue paper. Keep them dry and ventilated, and inspect everything regularly. Never expose them to sunlight, and keep them at normal domestic room temperature (between 40° and 80°F/4–27°C). Do not drop anything, not even plastic; carpeted floors are a safeguard.

TRANSPORTATION

Inevitably, from time to time a complete collection will need to be moved or quantities of figures taken from place to place. Travel arrangements mean fulfilling the storage requirements described above while on the move, and the trick is to prevent figures being rubbed or knocked in transit, with consequent damage to the paintwork, delicate parts or, in extreme cases, crushing or breakage.

When moving by hand in a situation when "this side up" can be enforced, a layer of soldiers covered with a layer of tissue and another layer of soldiers and so on will be sufficient. The interleaved nesting of the soldiers will keep everything safely in place, especially if the soldiers are laid out with fragile parts towards the centre. I often prefer to transport fragile plastic figures without tissue paper, simply wedged lightly into place by other figures. Len Richards used to sweep thousands of figures into a large Gladstone bag, saying that the weight would hold them steady and prevent movement without further precautions being necessary. Although I feel this to have been a little extreme, the principle is sound.

For transit by post or carrier, the first question to ask is, can it be avoided? Dealers and professional packers are usually adept at sending items by post, but even then accidents have been known to happen. If this sort of transit is unavoidable, it is worth taking trouble to sort out all soldiers of a similar weight. Solid lead figures can easily crush hollow-cast figures if they are in the same parcel, and hollow-casts can crush brittle plastics. Each figure should be wrapped, first in tissue to protect the paint, then in sufficient newspaper to protect fragile extremities. Stout, export-grade cardboard boxes will prevent the parcel being crushed, and firm packing within, using extra newspaper or wadding to fill the whole interior space, will prevent movement and damage as all the soldiers march up to the forward end of the parcel as it is slung against a warehouse wall.

11
MOUNTING AN EXHIBITION

Most collectors enjoy the opportunity to show their collections, and many of the subjects and cameos described in previous chapters are of interest not only to other collectors but also to the general public. To exhibit requires a great deal of effort and planning, but when it is over and the collection safely back home, it has always seemed to me the most rewarding occupation of all.

Here is a checklist of the things that need to be thought of before any exhibition is mounted:

1. Where is the exhibition to be held?
2. What is the occasion for, or purpose of, the exhibition?
3. Under whose auspices does the exhibition take place?
4. How long is there to get everything ready?
5. Who is to do what?
6. Will the exhibition be exposed to sunlight for long periods?
7. Can visitors touch the exhibits, and how can this be prevented?
8. How much room is available for display?
9. What figures will be needed to fill the room?
10. Is the exhibition to have a title?
11. For how long will the exhibition be on show?
12. For how long before the exhibition will the room be available for setting up?
13. Is access arranged?
14. Has a plan of the display been drawn up?
15. How firm is the base on which the models are to stand?
16. How good is the lighting?
17. Will the venue be ready beforehand or will extra clearing time be needed?
18. Has insurance been arranged and at whose cost?
19. How will the display be transported to the exhibition and at whose cost?
20. Is there to be associated written material – notices, handouts, catalogues, captions, etc? Who is to write the copy and who is to look after printing or lettering and at whose cost?
21. What are the arrangements for dismantling the exhibition? Is there a deadline?
22. Will help be needed with fetching and carrying or with security?

This array of bandsmen and Foot Guards at the slope (f) is spread out far too widely to give a good effect. The same troops, shown below, are better spaced, but the layout of the instruments is wrong – the drum, fife and bugle corps should be separated from the military band, and the men at the slope formed in another separate block, as one would normally see them in real life. *Phillips*

23. Is any remuneration involved or reimbursement of costs?
24. Are publicity arrangements to be made?
25. Can the exhibit be photographed for posterity?
26. Are souvenirs to be sold? If so, what and from where?

An exhibition of toy soldiers is one of the most attractive and appreciated displays that people can see but is much less commonly to be seen than, for instance, a model railway. As a result, for instance, following an exhibition of 4,000 figures put on at Gieves and Hawkes, London, in 1986, an item was shown on national television news three times, and pictures appeared in three daily papers as well as on a regional television feature programme. When publicity of this nature may be obtained, it is perfectly possible to arrange excellent venues in the windows of suitable shops and organizations, and, if they are professionally mounted, to be suitably reimbursed for the effort involved. For more modest occasions, one might arrange to put on a display in the window of a local building society in exchange for the opportunity to include a display card with a telephone number to ring if anyone who sees the display has old toys to dispose of.

The other major opportunity to put on a display is at a fete, carnival or other charity event, when organizers are usually keen to add interesting attractions to their programmes. This can either be on the basis of a free display, or else the space can be bought from the organizers and sales made from the table. If a game such as "guess the number of soldiers in a large box" is included, proceeds from this can go towards the charity.

Most charity events will either expect you to bring all your own display

When exhibiting in a shop window, uniforms and framed uniformed prints can be used to balance the extra height. Here, a mass of Britains cavalry appear on full dress field manoeuvres in the 1890s, with infantry defending the far end. Note the showcards giving information and the small caption blocks at the front.

equipment or else simply provide wobbly trestle tables, so be prepared. The venue may not even be indoors. Decide whether to display a selection of different figures or just have one big parade. Most of the time there will not be room to have more than one or two tables, 30in (76cm) by 6ft (1.8m), giving room for about 600 troops on each table. If you decide on a selection, portable shelves or showcases can be used to give more space. I like to cover the table with a grass green cloth wide enough to reach the floor. If you are going to these events regularly, a good investment would be a set of posts with a rope between them with which to keep the display out of reach of onlookers (at least 3ft/0.9m away), although it is not always possible to set this up, so check with the organizers about the width of gangways. Alternatively, a set of perspex sheets clamped to the front edge of the table will protect the display, although this does obscure the view.

This exhibition at Gieves and Hawkes, 1 Savile Row, London, was mounted in 1986. All sets of soldiers are keyed with a number mounted on a tiny wooden block for reference to the catalogue (and so that they can go back into the correct box). Eight abreast is a good size for a column and means that a set of Britains infantry can appear all in the same rank. *Press Association*

Setting up the exhibit is very time consuming unless there is some element of prefabrication. If soldiers have to be unpacked from paper and boxes and stood up in order, allow about an hour for 300 men. The more complicated the exhibition, the slower it will be to set everything out in order, particularly if, for instance, care has to be taken not to muddle similar sets with each other, and background material and captions have to be put in place. The exhibition with 4,000 figures mentioned above took 27 hours to set up. Any problems at all with access will add to the time. On one occasion I arrived to find that a previous exhibition had not yet been dismantled, and so lost half a day.

Prefabrication of an exhibition can save a great deal of time, however, and if the need is for an exhibition that will be mobile and quick to set out, it is possible to stick the infantry down to stiff card bases of a colour to match the layout cloth, using squares of double-sided sticky tape, which will peel away from the bases afterwards without much difficulty. If the cards are cut to the right size, a company of 40 men or more can stand upright in a shoe box. If it is necessary to prevent movement, suitably cut slabs of polystyrene foam can be wedged down the sides of the box. Cavalry and artillery are much harder to fix by this method, but there are likely to be fewer of them, and so setting up time can be cut by up to two thirds.

The more written material there is for an exhibition, the more impressive it will appear. Always caption everything, either next to the figures themselves or on a list keyed to the layout. A typewritten placard glued over an old showcard begged from any local shop (the sort that has a strut at the back to stand on a counter), is ideal for a start, and duplicated leaflets explaining the exhibit are not expensive. Exhibitions with catalogues will be remembered and enjoyed far more than those without. If the show is being arranged with any organization, even the local building society, suggesting a proper printed handout that will associate its name with yours will often bring a favourable response.

If you are putting items on display, remember to cross-reference any boxes for sets to their original contents. Small, sticky labels put under the bases of figures are a good idea. Many a collection has realized less than its full value at auction when two examples of the same set have been muddled on re-boxing, resulting in two mis-matched sets rather than two perfect ones. Once the two have each gone to different owners, they are almost irretrievable. This applies equally when selling duplicate sets: it is very annoying to discover later that the returned set is mismatched, so take care, and, if in doubt, take both sets for examination at the auctioneers.

12
COLLECTING AND INVESTMENT VALUE

Obviously most collectors have to budget their resources and suit their collecting to their means. There are, however, a few principles that are worth repeating here. First, go for the best items that you can afford. If prices go up, these will appreciate faster.

Second, go for the things that you personally like. You will have the pleasure of possessing them and enjoying their company, and, for value purposes, if *you* like them, it is the more likely that there will be others who will share your taste.

Third, if you come across one of the items that never appears on the market, stretch your resources to the limit to get it. Ed Ruby is fond of saying that "today's high price is tomorrow's bargain," and many of the things that he has bought over the years at what seemed then to be high prices have an incalculable value today because they have not appeared for sale again.

Britains set *318*, the rare set of the Royal Artillery gun team in khaki service dress, peak caps, at the halt, with gunners and officers, is shown with its original box (L).
Phillips

Finally, unless you want to be a dealer, avoid getting things because they appear to be cheap. Nine times out of ten there is a very good reason for it, and if they don't fit into your collection, they are no good to you.

Having said the above, it is true that in the period from 1970 to 1987, the value of toy soldiers at auction has risen steadily, and they have probably been as good an investment as almost any other over the same period.

INDEX OF VALUES

When production of Britains hollow-cast soldiers ceased in 1966, a single-row box cost 63p ($1.00) at Hamleys of Regent Street, London. Large and elaborate sets cost up to £5. When auctions started in 1969, boxed sets normally fetched between £3 and £10 each. By 1979, an average single-row box cost £30 to £50; by 1984, £70 to £100; and by 1987, £100 to £150. The more common sets are still available for £60 to £80 in their boxes. Unboxed sets or sets with defects sell for proportionately less. Rare items often reach over £1,000 – there were 20 such items in the January 1987 sale at Phillips, London, whereas in the comparable sale of May 1984 there had only been 11 such items.

RELATIVE EXPENSE OF THE MAJOR MANUFACTURERS

FLATS

Flats are generally inexpensive, and at British auctions they can go for as little as 20p a figure. However, very old (18th-century) or artistic figures, such as the work of *Allgeyer* or *Heinrichsen* in the manufacturers' original paint can cost some pounds per figure.

SOLIDS

Lucotte is one of the most expensive manufacturers to purchase, and £50 per figure is not unusual.

As *Mignot* is still in production, its figures are comparatively cheap compared with totally unobtainable old figures. However, when new, these figures cost about £75 for a box of 12 infantry or 6 cavalry, and at auction, since not all models are available new and the old painting is often rather more attractive, the price varies between £75 and £125.

The most common *Heyde* figures are the 48mm scale series, produced in an enormous variety of poses and finishes. Good boxed sets of 12 infantry, if attractive, go to £200 to £300 at auction. Often one can find Heyde figures in poor condition and with many of the delicate accessories missing for about £1 each, but these need a great deal of careful work to restore. Special displays of Heyde are rare, as are the larger scale figures. It is often difficult to distinguish between Heyde and the other German solid-cast manufacturers such as Heinrich and Haffner. As a rough guide, the more beautiful the figures, the more they are worth. The very lively set of field hospital figures from the Hanington collection, which comprised 93 pieces including four waggons, sold for £2,800 in 1984.

More modern equivalents of Heyde, such as *Brigadier* or the newly made *Potsdamer* sell for £5 to £8 per figure.

Some *Authenticast* figures and the subsequent *Swedish African Engineers* models are really splendid and command rather higher prices than the general line, which sell between £1.50 and £3 per figure. A neglected area of collecting, the 30mm scale Swedish African Engineers figures are extremely cheap, often 25p each. Other solid figures from the European countries are not widely collected, and depend for their price on their aesthetic qualities.

SEMI-FLATS

Semi-flat figures are rarely worth anything at all, but occasionally early examples with interesting moulding and paintwork can be worth reasonable amounts. A set of 34 pieces showing British Army medical services including a World War I motor ambulance fetched £150 at Phillips in November 1986.

HOLLOW-CAST FIGURES

The originator of the hollow-casting method, Britains, is the most expensive of the hollow-cast manufacturers to collect. The better, early sets of Britains with their boxes tend to cost from £400 to £600, and rare sets such as *set 148*, the Royal Lancaster Regiment, set up as a gameboard would sell for £3,000 to £4,000. Run-of-the-mill sets made in the 1930s and 1950s sell for between £70 and £200 for eight infantry or five cavalry. Individual figures generally vary from £4 to £20 if in very good condition, but there are large quantities of poorer condition, repainted or second-grade figures, which should not cost more than £1–2 apiece.

The imitators and competitors of Britains, in England, do not command the same high prices. Closest are the more attractive early figures of *B.M.C.* and *Reka*, which in boxed sets can reach £100 or over. Of the later figures, boxed sets of *Timpo* are well regarded, followed by *Hill*, and at the lower end, *Crescent*. These boxed sets range from £10 to £80. It is much more common to find these less collected figures loose, as indeed they were often originally sold, and their price as individual figures should not be more than £1 to £1.50 each unless particularly attractive.

DIME-STORE FIGURES

In the United States of America a whole sub-culture has appeared based around the products of *Barclay* and *Manoil*, 70mm scale hollow-cast figures, which were sold individually in "dime-stores" and are the American equivalent of the Hill and Crescent figures. They have a distinct style and charm of their own, and quite high prices can be paid for the rarer pieces. They are very rarely seen or collected outside America. Average prices range from $3 to $20 a figure, but have been known to reach $1,200.

RIGHT

This typical box contains lower quality, semi-flat early German toy soldiers, 45mm scale, and vehicles made of thin metal and tinplate. This sort of cheap toy soldier is far less likely to survive than the better quality, which tended to be treasured, but it has more curiosity value than any real aesthetic attraction (**H**). *Phillips*

OPPOSITE ABOVE

Britains set *1339*, the Royal Horse Artillery gun team with officer and four mounted gunners, all in khaki with steel helmets, is in its original box. Until 1940, this set was made with men wearing peak caps. Then, for a short period, along with other, similar horse-drawn vehicles, Britains manufactured them with the men wearing steel helmets. This extremely rare set sold at Phillips, London, for £7,200 in January 1985 (**M**). *Phillips*

OPPOSITE BELOW

Britains set *1450*, the Royal Army Medical Corps ambulance in khaki, has men in steel helmets, and set *1331*, the Royal Engineers General Service limbered waggon, has a driver in a steel helmet. As with the gun team illustrated above, these are extremely rare (**M**). *Phillips*

BELOW

Mignot solid-cast historical figures form a colourful group of crusading knights and men at arms, which were manufactured in France about 1950. Mignot is still producing similar toys, and they cost about £10 each (**f**). *Phillips*

COMPOSITION FIGURES

Elastolin and *Lineol* figures made of composition on wire frames have gained a worldwide collecting following. The most typical products were German Army of the World War I and World War II eras, but there were wide ranges of troops of various nations, and extensive selections of Nazi party figures and personalities, which are now much sought after and highly priced as a consequence. Typical single figures vary from as low as £3 to as high as £100 each. The tinplate vehicles made to accompany the 70mm scale figures are intricate and beautiful toys in their own right, and range from £300 upwards into four figures. Scales smaller than 70mm are generally much less expensive:

ALUMINIUM FIGURES

Wend-Al aluminium figures are not sought after or highly priced, but the French equivalents by *Quiralu* are beginning to be valuable to French collectors who now collect them. Only exceptional *Wend-Al* figures are worth over £1, but Quiralu can fetch up to £10 each.

PLASTIC FIGURES

Plastic figures are now becoming collectable, and some are already quite valuable, for instance the Herald English Civil War figures, a mounted one being worth up to £15. Plastics have to be in perfect condition and are usually not more than £2 each, although good Herald and Britains boxed sets can work out at considerably more per figure if they are the rarer varieties.

RARITY, DESIRABILITY AND AVAILABILITY

What determines the price of toy soldiers? In my experience, there are three main variables that set the market price. Rarity is the first, and this is a function of how many were originally made, how widely they were distributed in the market and how many have survived. Rarity is a rather theoretical consideration, which one might try to connect with the number of years that an item was on offer in the Britains catalogue. For instance, one would assume that the Servian and Montenegrin Infantry, which were not in the catalogue after 1934, would be rarer than the Bulgarian Infantry which remained in until 1939.

Linked to rarity is availability, which is simply the impression one gets that a particular item comes up for sale with a certain regularity. One might categorize most Britains sets along the lines "often, sometimes, seldom or never". The price fetched by items that turn up often and sometimes, however, are more determined by their popularity among collectors than by the frequency with which they are on offer. *Set 28*, Mountain Artillery for example, usually appears several times in every auction, but fetches around £150 to £250 a set at the time of writing, whereas the state coach, possibly a more imposing item, which turns up with much the same regularity, tends to fetch only £100 to £150.

Popularity among collectors is set to a degree by the patterns in which collections are assembled, and there are the popular subjects to collect – bands, colour parties, horse-drawn vehicles and so forth – which mean a higher price is usually reached by these than their rarity or availability would normally warrant. Salvation Army Bands and *set 2113*, the Band of the Grenadier Guards, are in the "sometimes" category of availability, which might mean two or three times a year. The price for these items in good condition is usually now £1,000 or more, which makes them more expensive than most items in the "seldom" category – i.e., those that are likely to come up less than once a year.

The age of toy soldiers from the time they were manufactured is to a degree important, but it may be outweighed by other factors, such as a very small number produced. Britains sets produced before 1916 tend to carry a premium price, and if they are in their original boxes could be up to twice the price normally paid for the same set manufactured later. Some sets, however, are expensive whenever they were made. The following lists outline the rare and desirable sets of Britains in three price ranges: very expensive (currently £2,000 to £5,000), fairly expensive (£1,500 to £3,000) and expensive (£700 to £1,500); *good* or better condition with original boxes is assumed.

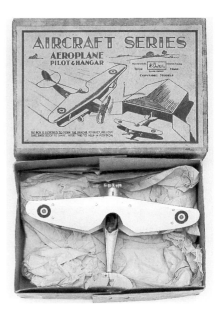

Britains *set 1521*, the Biplane, was the rarest production aircraft after the flying boat. Britains introduced the rounded end to the wings of its monoplane at this time also, but the biplane never had the earlier wing shape. To demonstrate the importance of a box: this example from the Hanington collection sold for £3,800 in 1984, while one without a box realized £2,200 in 1986 (**M**). *Phillips*

VERY EXPENSIVE
Set 39, Royal Horse Artillery Gun Team, first version with seated gunners
Set 72, Life Guards, Queen Victoria Jubilee souvenir set
Set 148, Royal Lancaster Regiment display tray game
Set 149, American soldiers display tray game
"Plug-handed" Fusiliers
"Plug-shouldered" Scots Greys
Gun teams at the halt
Horse-drawn vehicles with men in steel helmets
Set 1622, Band of the Royal Marine Light Infantry
Army Service Supply Column, distributed by C.F.E.
Set 1521, biplane
Set 1520, flying boat

FAIRLY EXPENSIVE
Set 1908, Infantry officers
Set 101, Band of the 1st Life Guards, "slotted arm" version, red or blue
Set 2113, Band of the Grenadier Guards
"Plug-shoulder" lancers, set of nine
Set 2093, Band of the Royal Berkshire Regiment
Set 2186, Band of the Bahamas Police
Any monoplane
Any autogiro
Boy Scout encampment sets
Set 1903, Indian Army Mountain Artillery
Salvation Army band, 17 or more pieces
Set 2014, Band of the U.S. Marines, winter dress

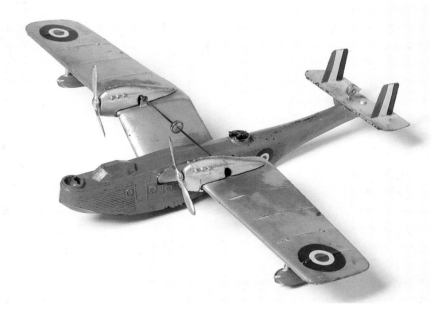

Britains set 1520, the Short Flying Boat, showing the original box (**M**). *Phillips*

RIGHT
All Britains aircraft are rare items, but set 1520, the Short monoplane flying boat is probably the rarest (**M**). It was sold at Phillips in 1982 for the lowish price of £1,100; it might now expect to fetch about £5,000. The body is made of Bakelite rather than the usual cast lead alloy fuselage found on Britains' other aircraft. The wings, which have a span of about 12in (30cm), are of tinplate. *Phillips*

OPPOSITE ABOVE
Britains set 2186, the famous and rare set of the Band of the Bahamas Police, was produced by Britains in 1959 specifically for sale in the Bahamas as a tourist souvenir. The set illustrated here, shown in a semi-scenic toy fort setting, was from the Richards collection (**L**). Britains is issuing a similar bugle band as its collectors' limited edition of die-cast models for 1987 (**B**). *Phillips*

OPPOSITE BELOW
Britains rare set 1903, the Indian Army Mountain Battery in khaki (**L**). Two mules have some carrying harness added. The full dress version of this set, produced after World War II, is even rarer (**M**). *Phillips*

Set 2110, Band of the U.S. Army, 25 pieces, yellow jackets
Set 2112, Band of the U.S. Marines, summer dress

EXPENSIVE
Set 2149, Gentlemen at arms
Set 37, Band of the Coldstream Guards, "slotted arm" version
Set 322, Drums and Fifes of the Coldstream Guards
Set 1721, Band of the Scots Greys, 12 pieces
Set 25, Soldiers to shoot
Set 2109, Pipe Band of the Black Watch
Set 211, 18in howitzer and 10-horse team
Set 144 or 144a, Royal Field Artillery
Any pontoon section set
Set 2184, Bahamas Police
Set 6, Boer Cavalry
Set 170, Greek Cavalry
Set 1749, barrage balloon with winch
Larger Britains buildings from the series in the 1940 catalogue
Set 1913, Cameronian Rifles
Set 98, King's Royal Rifle Corps, first version with spiked helmets
Sets 1556 to 1602, Regiments of the British Army
Set 255, The Green Howards

While the above is not a complete list of all the items that have ever been sold in the price ranges quoted, the listing includes all the well-known items that have been available on a regular or less frequent basis, and

From Britains *set 131*, a British Camel Corps figure (**m**). *Phillips*

equally those that tend to form the pride of any collection. In addition to these are the items that "never" appear – those things that are on offer so infrequently that I could only guess at their value. The very large boxed *sets 131* and *132* fall into this category. A partly complete box *131* with considerable damage and only in fair condition fetched £10,000 at Phillips in London in January 1987. Other large sets such as *set 73, set 129, set 1477* and *set 1555* tend to fetch much what one might expect from the figures that they contain, and so are still, given the added interest of having these figures contained in a large display box, a bargain.

"NEVER" ITEMS – i.e., those that may never be offered for purchase again.
Any boxed set of Paris Office figures
Set 131 or *132*
Any special paintings
Sets 10 and *14*, boxed set of first version Salvation Army figures
Sets 438 to *459, 479* to *490*, any parade series figures
Sets 1391, 1394 and *1397*, cardboard model fort or display box containing same
Any set number that never appeared on offer in the regular trade catalogue

Because so much of the toy soldier market comprises Britains figures, it is difficult to make up similar listings or highlights for the other manufacturers.

WHAT IS IT WORTH?

There is only one way to get a good idea of the current prices of toy soldiers, and that is to get as many lists and catalogues of items for sale as possible and learn them. Although when it comes down to it any of us who really want something will probably pay a high price for it if we can afford it, nevertheless it is as well to know what the generally accepted market value is. As with everything else, the price on any day is that at which one person is prepared to buy and another person is prepared to sell, so what is needed is some independent yardstick by which such a transaction can be measured, and it is here that the auctions, where the price is set by collectors in competition with each other, play a very useful part.

WHAT IS THE CHEAPEST WAY TO COLLECT?

How much time and money to spend on a collection is up to the individual collector, but time and money are to a degree interchangeable. The cheapest way is to search endlessly in antique and junk shops, canvass friends and relatives, advertise and watch for advertisements. This does take time, but in the long run may well produce bargains. Collecting in this way will certainly be slow, and much of what is acquired may not be what one wants to add to one's collection.

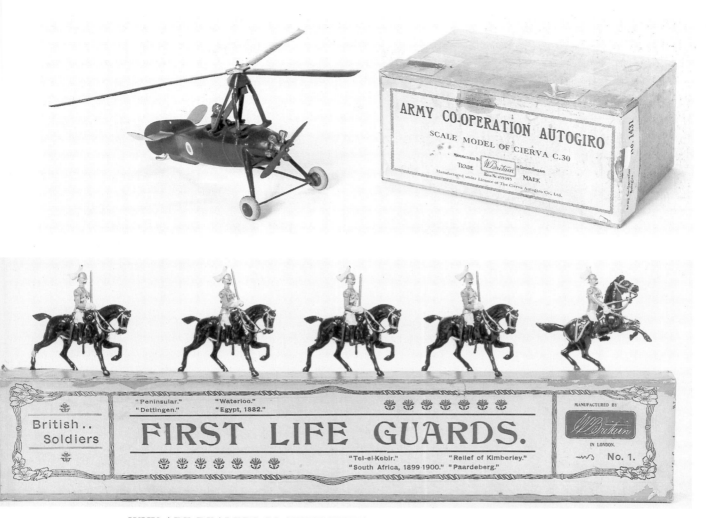

WHY ARE DEALERS SO EXPENSIVE?

Buying purely from specialist dealers would probably be the most expensive way to build up a collection, but consider also the advantages. The dealer has a large choice of items, from which you can buy exactly what you want. Many dealers take the trouble to pack expertly and dispatch goods by post worldwide, a service usually done for a nominal charge hardly if at all more than the postage involved. The dealer's expert knowledge is at your disposal, in that he has identified and sorted the item on offer and can often enlarge your knowledge of the importance of your purchase. All reputable dealers, furthermore, will back their service with a "no questions asked" money back guarantee. Although many people would consider dealers to be expensive compared with some other methods of collecting, bargains may be found on their lists, especially when it is a single figure that you have been wanting for a long time. In an

ABOVE
Britains set 1, the 1st Life Guards, seen here in its third version, which was made about 1908 (**G, g**). What is especially fascinating about the set is the vast number of different styles of box labels that were used; I have eight different examples, but not this one. *Phillips*

TOP
Britains set 1431, the Army Autogiro – an interesting piece of equipment made in the mid-1930s (**L**). *Phillips*

auction, the same figure might cost you less, but in all likelihood you would have had to have bought many other figures to get it, so the actual cash outlay would have been a lot more.

WHY DO AUCTION PRICES VARY?

Even when a succession of identical lots is put up at auction, their prices may vary. This may be because collectors fancy that they can detect some difference in quality, or it may be that postal bidding is heavy on some lots and not others. Some collectors like to bid for the early lots in a succession, some like to wait until later. When a set appears frequently at auction, the price will tend to remain fairly constant for similar quality, and reflect general rises and falls in the market, but there are always exceptions to this when two people in the auction room decide that they are prepared to go higher.

WHAT IS A FAIR PRICE?

There is only one person who can say what is a fair price, and that is you. If you are satisfied with the amount of money that you have expended on something, then that is a fair price, even if you see the same thing on sale for half the price 10 minutes later. Unless you also want to deal, the price at which you buy something needs only to correspond with your ability to pay. I have found that following my personal guidelines of what intrigues me, brings back memories or looks good to me has rarely let me down.

HOW SHOULD A COLLECTION BE VALUED?

There are three main methods of valuing a collection: the price it was bought for, the price it ought to fetch on re-sale, and the price it would cost to replace. It would be usual to allow an additional 50 per cent between the latter two figures, and in any case, it would be unlikely that, should a collection be lost for any reason, it would ever be able to be replaced exactly in every particular. The amount for which a collection is insured, therefore, is very much a matter of taste and how high a premium can be afforded.

BELOW AND OPPOSITE BELOW
Compare the Renvoize South Australian Lancers (**H, h**) with Britains set *49* (**J, k**). Renvoize offered its set with a trumpeter as an added bonus, making six figures compared with Britains' five. *Phillips*

PRICE GUIDE

The caption for each set or figure illustrated in this book includes a letter from A to M (sets) or a to m (figures) indicating the price range of that particular item. Auction prices can, of course, vary widely, but the price range given here is an indication of the relative value of each piece or set. Where both upper and lower case letters are included, the lower case letter refers to individual pieces from the set shown. Condition is assumed to be *good* or better in all cases (see pages 60–8).

A less than £20	a less than £1	H £200–£400	h £16–£25
B £20–£50	b £1–£2	I £300–£600	i £20–£40
C £40–£70	c £2–£4	J £500–£1000	j £35–£60
D £60–£90	d £3–£5	K £1000–£2000	k £50–£80
E £80–£120	e £4–£8	L £1500–£3000	l £70–£100
F £100–£150	f £7–£12	M more than £2500	m more than £100
G £150–£250	g £10–£18		

SELECT BIBLIOGRAPHY

I recommend here those books (including those by myself) that I have found the most useful for research.

Model Soldiers: A Collector's Guide, John G. Garratt, Seeley, Service
The late John Garratt's original book on model soldiers remains the classic work on the early history of both models and toys. It is out of print but can be found second-hand.

The World Encyclopedia of Model Soldiers, John G. Garratt, Muller, London, 1981
At a later date, John Garratt incorporated a great deal more information into this alphabetical listing and critique of model and toy soldiers. The listing of manufacturers is excellent, and the appendices include lists of public displays by country, an exhaustive bibliography and thematic indices by country of origin, and method of manufacture. Recently out of print.

Little Wars, H. G. Wells, first published in 1913
A famous classic of early war-gaming, the illustrations of the Britains toy soldiers used by H.G.W. are of themselves worth obtaining a copy. Facsimile editions are easy to obtain. The rules used are still unsurpassed for simplicity, fairness and excitement, although not many modern players would use original Britains with fully loaded spring guns.

Regiments of all Nations, Joe Wallis, privately published U.S.A.
This is an unrivalled work of research, listing as it does all Britains lead figures from 1946 to 1966. Illustrations are in black and white, but the store of knowledge is an almost complete survey of the subject, and as such should be on the shelf of anyone attempting to collect from this period of Britains production.

Britains Toy Soldiers 1893–1932, James Opie, Gollancz, London. Harper & Row, New York, 1985
In this book I attempted to list and discuss all Britains military figure production for the period specified. Illustrated with 64 pages of colour and arranged by collecting theme, it is my major contribution towards the study of a manufacturer in depth.

The Britains Collector's Checklist, Joanne and Ron Ruddell, privately published in three volumes, U.S.A., 1980–2
Although there is no major book as yet on the period of Britains production from 1932 to 1941, these listings, which include information of nearly all the sets issued from 1893 to 1966, go far to cover the gap. When Donald Pudney publishes the *Britains Ltd Master List of Toy*

Soldiers and Models, which are extracted from Britains own factory records, more will be known about this period.

A Collector's Guide to Britains Model Soldiers, John Ruddle, Model and Allied Publications, 1980
This is a comprehensive listing of all of Britains production, with useful commentary and excellent pictures – but look out for printers' errors.

Toy Soldiers, James Opie, Shire Publications, Princes Risborough, 1983
This was my first book, intended as an inexpensive introduction to the hobby. Useful to give to people who would like to understand in outline what the field of toy soldiers is, and saves hours of explaining to friends.

Toy Armies, Peter Johnson, Batsford, London, 1982
This very readable book is primarily based around the Forbes Museum collection of toy soldiers, of which Peter Johnson is the curator, but it also contains a great deal of other interesting information.

Collecting Old Toy Soldiers, Ian McKenzie, Batsford
This was the first book to treat old toy soldiers on a par with models and specifically separate the two hobbies.

The Collector's All Colour Guide to Toy Soldiers, Andrew Rose, Salamander
An excellent book of large-size colour photographs of a miscellany of toy soldiers representing most of the main types. Many of the figures are from two of England's most noted collectors, Edmund Roche-Kelly and Peter Cowan.

Old British Model Soldiers 1893–1918, Len Richards, Arms and Armour Press, London, 1970
This was the classic early illustrated book of toy soldiers by the pioneer of systematic toy soldier collecting. Now out of print.

British Toy Soldiers 1893 to the Present, James Opie, Arms and Armour Press, London, 1985
In this book I supplemented the previous work of Len Richards with a wider range of toy soldiers and a full price guide.

Books specializing in certain toy soldier fields are:
The War Toys (Kriegsspielzeuge): No 1, the story of Hausser-Elastolin, Reggie Polaine, New Cavendish Books, London
Model Tin Soldiers, Erwin Ortmann, Studio Vista, London
This is about flat figures
The Barclay Catalog Book, Richard O'Brien

BACKNUMBERS OF AUCTION CATALOGUES
These are available from Phillips Auctioneers, 7 Blenheim Street, London W1Y 0AS, England. Particularly useful are the highly illustrated ones I wrote for the Richards collection, the Hanington collection and that of January 1987, which included the Morris collection; price £5 each.

MAGAZINES AND PERIODICALS

These are important for up-to-date news of research, items for sale, events and newly issued models and toys.

The Old Toy Soldier Newsletter, 209 North Lombard, Oak Park, IL 60302, U.S.A.
This is the first toy soldier magazine, and majors on research and information articles. Six issues a year by subscription.

Toy Soldier Review, 127 74th Street, North Bergen, N.J. 07047, U.S.A.
A more glossy quarterly, this magazine includes chatty pieces about collectors and collecting. By subscription and available from some dealers.

Bulletin of the British Model Soldier Society published since 1935.
This includes more about models than toys, but the society caters for both. By subscription to society membership: I. Webb, 35 St John's Road, Chelmsford, Essex, England.

Communiqués of the Toy Soldier Collectors of America
Very useful for getting in touch with other collectors. By subscription to the society: John Giddings, 6923 Stone's Throw Circle # 4202, St. Petersburg, Florida 33710, U.S.A.

Collectors Gazette
Enquiries for subscription to: Ms Elaine Hill, 17 Adbolton Lodge, Whimsey Park, Carlton, Nottingham, England. This monthly broadsheet gives details of swapmeets throughout the U.K. with reviews of models and auctions, and carries many collectors' and dealers' advertising, for all types of toys.

"On Guard" Toy Soldier Exhibition Catalogue, New Cavendish Books, London
This is the catalogue for my exhibition at the London Toy and Model Museum, 23 Craven Hill, London W2 3EN, and copies are still available from the museum.

Plastic Warrior, Paul Morehead, 65 Walton Court, Woking, Surrey, England.
This newsletter is for collectors, convertors and war-gamers in 54mm scale plastic figures.

Mignot-Lucotte Historical Review, Don Grant, PO Box 5, San Luis Obispo, California 93406, U.S.A.
A learned review of the past output of these two associated French manufacturers.

INDEX